Spiritual Songs:

LETTERS FROM MY CHEST

Ann Marie Ruby

ISBN: 0692852271
ISBN-13: 978-0692852279

DEDICATION

This is a special book from my soul. I have seen people looking for some kind of spiritual guidance. That is why we have different religions and faiths all around this globe. I believe religions speak of peace and are a guidance.

As a spiritual person, I have found this peace in my heart. When I speak to those of whom affiliate with a religion and those of whom with no religious affiliation, all are talking about their own beliefs so strongly only to put down the other person standing next to us. I do not know why, but my inner soul cries for all humans. All we need to do is be kind. This requires no effort, just like the pure laugh of a baby, how it rejuvenates the soul. May we all find in ourselves the complete innocence to give the gift of kindness.

I pray for all humans to find peace amongst ourselves and receive all as the children of The Creator. As I like to say my own quote, "Let us the judged not be The Judge." I remind myself, The Lord created every single one of us and must have a plan for each one of us. In The Lord's own time, The Lord will share. Until then, may we all be in peace as one family.

Let there be peace amongst us and may The Lord guide all. Until then, let us find spiritual awakening and simple songs to share amongst all of The Lord's creation, a theme song of union of all race, color, and religion. We love The Creator, for we are the creation.

I have written spiritual songs, prayers from my soul, worshiping The Creator. How much we all love The Creator, we get emotional and fight over this as to who is right or who is wrong. From beginning of time until the end of time, we have one thing in common, we love The Creator.

The skies, the oceans, the Earth, and the Heavens above we all love. The creation we are, standing on this Earth which never changes, as all that changes is we the creation. As I wrote in my book *Spiritual Travelers: Life's Journey From The Past To The Present For The Future*, "The land, the sky, and all of this nature stand still, for all that moves is the human. The Artist of the canvas, and the true beauty of The Lord remain steadfast always there, for me today, and you tomorrow."

My prayer for all is may we find in our heart the pure love for all souls and not become an enemy, but a friend as we worship in our own ways. Please find these prayers written from my soul as a gift for all spiritual beings and a motivation for union. We can worship different ways, but love The Creator as one, for we are the creation.

Songs of life, I call them as they bring sweet love of kindness, tears of joy, and harmony to all humans. May my tears be the tears of union. Let us join hands and let the neighbors worship as they please and find the common ground to love all as The Creator is one and so are the creation.

As we enjoy the sunset, the sunrise, the birth, or death of a neighbor, may there be peace, serenity, and harmony. The Earth is so beautiful where and when there is love. When and where there are struggles, despair, fear, and hatred, may these spiritual songs give you what is needed to heal your soul.

Medication you can take to heal your physical pain and may these meditative spiritual songs be the healer of your emotional pain. As I wrote in my book *Spiritual Travelers: Life's Journey From The Past To The Present For The Future*, "Physical pain treated through medication, emotional pain treated through meditation."

May we heal each other with love and joy, far beyond our times. May we create a future for all humans to be in peace as The Creator has created all of us with so much love.

I dedicate this book to all of whom seek peace and harmony. Please accept these prayers as a gift from a stranger, who also wants to be a friend. In union, let us fight for each other, not against each other.

I dedicate this book to four very special individuals I have known along this journey of life, who stood by me throughout everything, watched my tears fall, and shared laughter and joy with me. Whenever I saw darkness, they appeared like a candle. When I was soaked in the rain, they became my umbrella. For them, I am here today, tomorrow, and will be always as our soul lives on eternally.

I dedicate this book to the four, who know whom they are, but wish to remain unknown and want to be just there. I admired them yesterday, today, and tomorrow. You know I will keep your names in my soul forever. May the world find people like you all around the universe as they need a helping hand.

A stranger today, a friend forever tomorrow. I call these strangers we bump into my Guiding Angels. You four are my Guiding Angels. I love you forever. Like four corners, may you be the bridge of union for all humans. Spread love and know the tears I spread for my Lord is all my love for The Creator and the creation.

INTRODUCTION

Life is a gift we land upon. The journey spreads throughout memory lane. At times, we follow the footprints left behind. At other times, we are left to create our own footprints. All along the journey, we try to help each other as we travel to our destination. I have written spiritual songs as my solace through this journey. I have given them as friendship bread from my basket to all of whom seek spiritual awakening.

From sunrise to sunset, and throughout the dark nights, may my spiritual songs be a friend to those in need. With love, peace, and harmony, let us walk upon the blessed Earth as one family. I have written these songs from my heart to yours. May my spiritual songs find a place in your heart, as they have given me peace. As I carry them in my basket, I find love for all creation of my Lord.

The love and union between all creation is possible through spiritual awakening. The spiritual rejuvenation calms the inner soul, as then we awaken to find inner peace. The journey of life comes with its own course as it lands upon our doors. Each door has its own path and differences between them. I have built a bridge of union between all different race, color, and religion called spiritual awakening. For the love of all humans, I have learned to live with our differences in harmony through spiritual awakening. Our paths may be different. Our ways of life separate us, but the love for all of you unites my heart to each and every soul born or to be born. With each heartbeat, let us unite and sing the songs of life. In sickness or in health, let us be there for each other. As spiritual souls, we are all one family. Anger, pain, and war hurt, so why not spread love and joy all around the Earth?

Spiritual awakening bridges all different cultures together and throughout eternity. Let us be awakened through our spiritual journey. For my spiritual family, I have written these songs as a gift from my soul to yours. Be my family for even with all the differences, may we shine in the sky like a beautiful rainbow. I love you all. My gift for all of you are the songs from my spiritual journey, the prayers from my heart, *SPIRITUAL SONGS: LETTERS FROM MY CHEST*.

*This book is not affiliated with any religious group, religious view, or religious perspective. This is a complete spiritual book of spiritual prayers. It is for anyone who needs motivation, spirituality, inspiration, love, wisdom, guidance, and hope, for all humans regardless of your religious affiliation. I believe there is a Creator, and we are but the creation.

MESSAGE FROM THE AUTHOR

May there be peace amongst all, as we awaken spiritually and be the hope of peace for all. Religion is a sacred, spiritual journey everyone takes upon his or her awakening. Life brings different religions to different doors and knocks with different sounds. The House of Christianity – the church bells ring, The House of Judaism – its Barechu, The House of Islam – the Adhan, and The House of Hinduism – the temple bells ring as all gather up for union.

I pray for peace as there are so many faces who do not fit into any of the houses. Are they then homeless? No, I think they belong in this House of Union, where all race, color, and religion gather and stand together as we the children know we are the creation and You, my Lord, are but The Creator. Through the journey of life, we collect knowledge to leave behind for the future generations.

I call all of whom want to spread the knowledge of peace, a messenger. The Lord knows all that but remains unknown to us, as we fight amongst ourselves declaring who is mightier. I remain blessed with the knowledge, all of The Lord's creation are the best, for how can they not be? For is it not my Lord who created all of us? The Creator has created all of the creation with so much love. For this, we are the blessings of my Lord.

May all the creation awaken spiritually from our inner soul and be the peace we all are looking for. Be the giver of peace, be the one who brings peace, be the cause of union amongst all race, all color, and all religion. Be yourself and worship that within which your soul but finds peace.

In union, let us recite, "Let us the judged not be The Judge." Be spiritual and waken from inside. Motivate all to do good, spread love, be kind, and show kindness to the strangers. All we the humans but want is peace within this one world. May The Creator see all of us and judge us as we complete this journey.

I do not ever want to condemn a soul for his or her race, color, or religion for it hurts too much. I watch all and think to myself how can I, my Lord, be in Heaven if Your creation is condemned for their beliefs? They have tried according to their ways and teachings they have landed upon. How do we walk alone and leave all behind? The Creator knows what is not known to me, but love comes from The Creator who has created all. A child had once asked me, "So do all Christians go to Heaven? Or do the Muslims? Or do the Jews? Or is it the Hindus? Who goes to Heaven and who does not?"

I had no answer and as I left for home, I wondered what truly happens. I thought again, "Let us the judged not be The Judge." I thought to myself I shall do good and be good. I shall awaken spiritually from inside for I love this Earth and all upon this Earth. I prayed for all creation of The One Creator as I became a vegetarian not for religion, but because of my love for all creation. For me, spiritual awakening in itself was a complete blessing. The truth is as days pass by, they never come back. They only leave behind messages from the past. As I pick up the messages, I know we the creation must unite for peace and love.

Love is a strange word as you might think I have conquered love. I have teardrops as my life partner. I have enough teardrops to wash my inner soul with every day. I started to write my inspirational quotations as they helped me through this journey of life. As my book of inspirational quotations came out, a stranger wrote to me, "You don't know how much these words have helped me." I read and realized one of my Lord's creation has found peace through my words, blessed be.

I have chosen my Lord as my love, and I write prayers from my soul for my Lord. I call them spiritual songs, as with my mind, body, and soul, I sing them for my Lord. They have helped me through this journey of life. Love was a word lost to me until I realized love is not lost for just as I have given all my love to my Lord, I can give my love to all, even those of whom ask and those of whom do not ask. I shall leave the songs at the doors and if they help, consider them all my love for you.

These are songs of prayers from my heart. They can be a friend in all of the houses across this globe. Find the innermost peace through spiritual awakening. Spread peace and become the first one to be the helping hand in disguise. I know we are the worshippers of The Worshiped, the creation of The Creator. How can we the creation not love each other as we all love our Creator? Spread love and bring love back to your soul.

With love, I give you from my heart,

SPIRITUAL SONGS:
LETTERS FROM MY CHEST

TABLE OF CONTENTS

LETTERS FROM MY CHEST

My Lord, my Creator,

My mind, my body, and my soul

Only worship You.

My Lord, my Creator,

May all my prayers,

All my blessings,

All my love be only for You,

Always be hidden away from all evil,

Away from all harm.

May my words not be loud trumpets.

May my world not be for the riches.

May my prayers be

From a creation to The Creator,

LETTERS FROM MY

CHEST.

GLORY BE TO MY LORD

My Lord, as dawn breaks open

Through the night sky,

May I, Your devotee, only worship You.

My Lord, with this first sight of light,

May I, Your devotee, only worship You.

My Lord, after the dark night's struggle,

The sparkling array of the morning light

Glorifies the Earth.

On this day, may I, Your devotee,

Only worship You.

My Lord, as the sun reaches through

To each and all of Your creation,

May we, the creation, say in union,

"GLORY BE TO MY LORD."

GUIDING LIGHTS

Oh my Lord up in Heaven,

Grace our day with Your blessings

As the morning comes

With the sun shining through the skies.

May Your blessings befall on us

Through every breath and sigh.

May the day bring joy and laughter

Throughout every household on Your Earth.

May the footsteps of all Your creation

Reach Your Door.

When the night befalls on us,

May Your moon and shining stars

Guide the lost and stranded souls.

At the End of Time, may we be guided Home

To You, my Lord,

By Your

GUIDING LIGHTS.

MY PATH

My Lord The Almighty,

May my path always lead me to Your Door.

Lord Almighty, You alone I cry upon.

My Lord, I walk upon Your Path alone.

Alone in the dark,

I shall walk with You as my Guide,

Your moon as my guide during the dark nights,

With Your hope in my twinkling eyes.

During the daylight hours,

I shall pray to You on my knees

For all Your creation to find You

And be on Your Path.

Your Path, may it always shine with Your Light

Guiding all onto it.

May all see the love of The Lord Almighty.

May all be filled with the joy and pride

As they travel upon Your Path.

The pain and tears I shed on This Path

Be only for You and be only mine.

My Lord,

For You, I say the truth,

For You, I shall lay my life.

May my path always take me to You.

My Lord, may my path be blessed upon.

May The Gates of Heaven

Be open to all on This Path,

May Your blessed Path always be

MY PATH.

THE TRAVELERS

I the traveler walk upon my journey.

The heated sun burns, blazing my skin.

The cold shivering chills of the freezing nights

Blister my skin.

I still am glad for I know this pain is nothing

For I have the glad tidings of my Lord

On This Path.

This Path, The Path to Heaven is all I want.

I see many travelers on the journey

Whom I bump into along the way.

Busy they are with the pleasures of life.

Women and men find comfort in each other,

Hiding from the cold nights as a one night stand.

People missing work for

They want to escape the blazing sun.

Escape you may today from the fire and cold,

But tomorrow at The Lord's House,

You shall burn and freeze eternally.

I teach them my Lord along the way,

Give glad tidings to your Lord and walk upon

His Road even though hard it may seem.

For this hardworking Road

Will take you to The Eternal Peace.

On The Road of The Lord,

You will find your true blessings.

These blessings may come hard,

But will take us to our Final Destiny.

The traveler I am, seeking to please my Lord.

Sacrifice I commit is but all my love for my Lord.

No sacrifice is but a sacrifice

For my Lord has a House ready upon my arrival,

Where no fire shall burn me,

Nor cold shall touch me,

Nor any misery shall befall.

For my Lord has The House ready

For those of us whom make the journey,

THE TRAVELERS.

THE HOUSE OF MY LORD

My Lord up in Heaven,

Keep me on Your Path.

May The Lord's blessings

Fall upon The Road I travel on.

May Your blessings

Keep all evil away from me at all times.

May no evil follow me, touch me, or make me sin.

Oh my Lord, I take the oath to be

On Your Path of Truth and Justice for all times.

May I also be merciful to all

As You are The Most Merciful.

May I be on Your Path as an example

Of Your true devotee.

Guide me, protect me my Lord

As I set out to do my job.

Bless my Path forever

So through This Path, I may guide myself

And all of whom seek the direction unto

Your House,

THE HOUSE OF

MY LORD.

TEARDROPS OF MY LORD

The sky is clouded with dark clouds,

Raindrops pouring all over the lands.

My Lord, why are You crying?

I pour my teardrops for You, my Lord,

Longing to do the right by You, my Lord.

I want to follow The Path of Your footsteps.

I wish to show all Your creation

The Door to Your Home.

Even if my walk on Your Path

Seems never ending,

May my tired soul never get off This Road.

My love for You, my Lord, is so strong.

I feel Your pain for all Your children.

My Lord, I hear You call

All Your children to come Home.

My Lord, You stand at The Door

Waiting for all Your children,

Praying to never let a single soul get off

The Right Path.

I, Your child, keep disappointing You, my Lord.

I, Your child, promise to guide

Your children Home to You,

For I, Your child, can take all the pain

Mother Earth can give me,

But not the

TEARDROPS OF

MY LORD.

BRING THE CHILDREN HOME

Oh my Lord, guide me on this treacherous road.

The Path is there, the guidelines are here.

My Lord, tell me how do I get all

Your children on This Road?

If only my Lord,

They would open their eyes, hearts, and souls,

They could see their Lord is but waiting for

All to come Home.

My Lord, please give me the strength

To pull one by one on This Road.

My Lord, give me the courage to say

The unwanted truth they do not want to hear.

My Lord, make me all merciful like You

So I can take their anger filled hate

And still bless them.

My Lord, make me shine like all

Your shining stars
Who have been lighting The Path
For all throughout time,
So I may show them The Right Path and
BRING THE CHILDREN
HOME.

THE HEALER

My Lord, The Healer, The Omni,

Heal this Earthly body of Your creation.

This world has given illness and

Bedridden Your devotees.

The soul is as always pure and clean.

The Earthly body cries in pain,

Heart cries for You,

Wants to just be in devotion of You.

Earthly body does not move

For it is in pain my Lord.

Cure Your true devotees

For You are The Ultimate Truth.

May we never leave Your Path

Even if our mind leaves us out of illness.

May our pain and sickness

Be wiped away by Your love.

May our prayers reach Your Door.

Heal us for we cry only to You.

Sickness and in health,

We ask You to never leave us.

Oh my Lord,

I know You are The Only One I cry upon,

For You are The Ultimate Truth,

THE HEALER.

FOREVER AND EVER

For You, my Lord, I strive.

For You, my Lord, I live my life.

For You, my Lord, tears roll from my eyes.

For You, my Lord, I wake up in sighs.

For You, my Lord, everything I will give.

For You, my Lord, I hold all this.

For You, my Lord, the world but is.

For You, my Lord, I but am.

For You, my Lord, I just stand

High up on the mountain looking down.

In Your love, I will drown.

All the pain and sorrow I put away

For I know we meet few hours away.

Oh my Lord, I wait just for You.

Prayers I recite all but for You.

I come to You, my Lord,

Flying like the pure white dove,

FOREVER AND EVER.

LIFE ON THIS EARTH IS BUT A DAY

My Lord The Most Merciful,

I seek forgiveness in You from all sins of this day.

May my day be filled with Your mercy.

May I be only on Your Path throughout my day.

May I be an example of Your true devotee.

May my prayers reach Your Door my Lord.

May the mornings be glorified

With Your blessings my Lord.

May the sun shine throughout every household

On this Earth in Your name my Lord.

May all Your creation know of their Lord,

The Omnipotent, before night falls my Lord.

May all of Your children know my Lord,

LIFE ON THIS EARTH IS

BUT A DAY.

ASK AND I SHALL FORGIVE

My Lord The Most High,

I the sinner cry up to the sky.

In search of You,

I climb mountains which reach the sky.

I cross oceans after oceans in sigh.

Oh my Lord, my heart filled with guilt as

I have sinned up to the sky.

Oh my Lord, guide me to You,

Take me back on Your Path I cry.

My Lord, I will walk thousands of miles

In search just of You.

Everywhere I lay my eyes in search just for You.

Forgiveness I ask not of You

But to pull me into Your arms.

It is getting dark my Lord,

So I return home with a heavy heart.

Oh my Lord, my house is lighted up
With Your light.
Tears roll as I hear Your loving words,
"ASK AND I SHALL
FORGIVE."

KISS OF AN ANGEL

Oh my Lord, bless us

With courage, honor, and dignity

As we await the Angel of Death.

So gentle, so kind is his final kiss.

So soft are his fingers as he touches

All of Your creation.

He cries to You, my Lord, for Your creation,

"Fear me not, but fear your Lord. Ask your Lord

The Most Merciful for forgiveness.

The Lord shall answer."

Your Angel of Mercy repeats

Over and over to all of us.

My Lord,

May we, Your creation, only fear our sins.

May we be guided by You

And always be on Your Path.

My Lord,

At our final hour,

May we, Your Creation, only prove

Our love for our Lord.

May our love for You overcome all fear of death.

May we welcome The Merciful Angel of Death

As he comes to take us Your creation

Home to You.

So, we welcome with all our love, the merciful

KISS OF AN ANGEL.

MY LORD

Oh The Omnipotent, The Almighty,

The Omnipresence,

Let my heart not be filled

With anger and pride my Lord.

Let there be no regret and disgrace in me my Lord.

Let there be no jealousy

In this Earthly body my Lord.

Let this Earthly body be always sin free my Lord.

Let me thread The Road of

Your devotees my Lord.

Let there be love and warmth in my heart my Lord.

Let love and honor rule my path my Lord.

Let my eyes see only the truth my Lord.

Let my ears only hear love my Lord.

Let my hands only worship You, my Lord.

Let my feet only be on Your Path my Lord.

Let me, Your true devotee, be able

To find my way back to You, my Lord.

Let this human body always be in worship of You,

MY LORD.

LOVE AND PEACE

My Lord The Omnipresence,

The Creator of this world and beyond,

With so much love You have created everything.

Mother Earth shares her lap

To shelter all Your creation.

The sun and moon burn themselves to light us.

Twinkling stars in the night sky

Giving us free entertainment.

The wind blowing us fresh air.

All the rivers flowing to give us water to drink.

Trees bearing fresh fruit

And vegetation for our food.

My Lord, You have blessed us with Your love.

My Lord, Your love knows no boundary

And has no end.

With every breath,

You have loved us and taught us to love.

Today, I raise my hands in a prayer to You.

May we, Your creation, give and share

All that You have sent us.

May we learn to love all humans as our own kin.

May we learn to live on Your Earth

Until our departure in

LOVE AND PEACE.

DOOR TO HEAVEN

My Lord The Most Forgiving, The Most Loving,

I, Your most beloved devotee, wait

For You at the tunnel of life.

My Lord, the tunnel of life

Takes the shape of our character.

To the sinner, the tunnel of sin,

To the pious, the tunnel of peace.

My Lord, my baggage of sin

Burdens my shoulders.

I am ashamed trying to count

My good deeds my Lord.

Show me The Path of good deeds my Lord.

Forgive my sins my Lord as I am Your lost child.

Show me where and how

I can cleanse my soul my Lord.

I devote my life to You on Your Path my Lord.

Born again like a new baby,

I walk only for You, my Lord.

I hold my hands up in prayers my Lord

With each and every breath.

My Lord, I await Your call

At the end of my life.

My Lord, I shall walk with You

Through the tunnel of life.

My Lord, I know through this tunnel lies my

DOOR TO HEAVEN.

CALL UPON MY LORD THE OMNIPRESENCE

My Lord The Most High,

My Lord The Most Kind,

I call upon You, my Lord.

I come to You, my Lord.

With grief filled heart, I call You, my Lord.

All around me, darkness rolls my Lord.

Pain and sorrow fill the night sky my Lord.

Hands up high, I pray only to You, my Lord.

I walk on Your Path

Picking up thorns for Your devotees my Lord.

I give You my hands my Lord.

Hold my hands my Lord.

Walk with me my Lord.

I, Your true devotee, await Your arrival my Lord.

Oh my Lord The Most Loving,

Bless us with Your presence.

My Lord The Most Giving,

Grace our day.

Join us now for I

CALL UPON MY LORD

THE OMNIPRESENCE.

THE FOOTSTEPS OF OUR LORD

My Lord The Most Merciful,

The Most Humble, The Most Loving.

May You be victorious.

May You be victorious.

May You be victorious.

May our Lord be victorious.

May our Lord of all creation be victorious.

May You lead Your army of Angels, humans,

And all Your creation onto Your Path.

May we,

Your devoted Angels and devoted humans,

Join hands with each other.

May You lead Your Angels and humans to victory.

May we follow the footsteps of our Lord.

May Your footsteps be imprinted on Your Path.

May we, Your true devotees,

Be able to follow Your Path.

No evil shall enter This Path

For This Path is blessed with our Lord's footsteps.

Our Lord's footsteps lead us

Unto The Lord's Door

For This Door is the only entry

To The House in Heaven.

May we enter The House in Heaven

Through our Lord's footsteps.

Our Lord, You covered The Path You walked on

With Your teardrops.

Our Lord, Your teardrops light up

Your footsteps on Your Path.

Teardrops of our Lord purify our sins,

As we walk on the footsteps of our Lord.

So let us, all of the creation, follow

THE FOOTSTEPS OF

OUR LORD.

CONSORT OF LIFE IS DEATH

My Lord, accept my prayer of life.

Life is a circle which must meet her consort.

My Lord, I pray for my life

For it only lasts a day as dawn begins.

At the break of dawn, I pray for love.

Hold my hands my Lord

And take me to the early afternoon.

As the afternoon walks into my life,

I pray for courage.

I walk on my Lord's Path

Holding my Lord's hands as I end up at dusk.

Now my Lord, I pray for honor.

I can barely see my Lord

For dusk is becoming dark.

Hold my hands my Lord as I pray only to You.

My Lord, now I need You the most

For my path leads to dark nightfall.

I need my dignity

For I cannot see, or walk, or hear, or talk

For darkness engulfs all around.

My Lord, I know with Your holding hands,

I shall walk and cross this bridge of my life

For life has given me

Love, courage, honor, and dignity,

But now I give my life her consort for I know

My Lord, the

CONSORT OF LIFE IS

DEATH.

FORGIVENESS, REDEMPTION, AND AWAKENING

My Lord high up in The Heavens,

Your world has manifested in sins.

All around me,

Your creation have become full of sins.

Thus, dark souls surround me.

I walk amongst the sinners.

The sinners have made me into a sinner.

Forgive me my Lord.

Forgive me my Lord.

Forgive me my Lord.

My Lord, the souls of Your creation

Have become dark.

The rivers and the oceans are filled with sins.

The deep water is drowning me in the river of sins.

My Lord, I have become manifested with sins

For all around me,

There is nothing but waves of sins.

My Lord, with hands held up high,

I ask forgiveness for my sins.

My Lord, pull me up from the ocean of sins.

My Lord, forgive me.

My Lord, forgive me.

My Lord, forgive me.

My Lord, I am drowning in this ocean of sins

And I cannot come out of it for all around me,

Souls have become dark and dingy.

Pull me up for I see the shore.

I feel the mountain breeze.

I smell the spring water from the mountain.

Cleanse me my Lord with the mountain waters.

Pour the raindrops all over me.

Wash away my sins my Lord.

Cleanse me my Lord.

Cleanse me my Lord.

Cleanse me my Lord.

Forgive me my Lord.

Forgive me my Lord.

Forgive me my Lord

For sins have manifested

Into the deep waters of the ocean.

All around me, the waves of sins

Drown me my Lord.

Hold my hands my Lord.

Hold my hands my Lord.

Hold my hands my Lord

And pull me out of this ocean of manifested sins.

I am drowning my Lord.

I am drowning my Lord.

I am drowning my Lord.

I see my Lord upon the ocean

On top of a bed of water.

Sins flow in the water,

But the sins do not see or touch my Lord.

Forgive me my Lord.

Forgive me my Lord.

Forgive me my Lord for my manifested sins.

I will walk for my Lord

Through an ocean of poisonous sins.

The love for my Lord is so great,

No sin can touch me or drown me.

For my Lord, I shall give my life.

For my Lord, I shall give my life.

For my Lord, I shall give my life.

My Lord picks me up

From an ocean of sins.

No sin shall touch me.

No dark, dingy soul shall come near me

For we, the creation, ask and my Lord forgives.

My Lord calls upon all the creation.

It is time we, the creation, ask for

FORGIVENESS, REDEMPTION,

AND AWAKENING.

FORGIVENESS, REDEMPTION,

AND AWAKENING.

FORGIVENESS,

REDEMPTION, AND

AWAKENING.

DEVOTION OF MY LORD

I, the sinner, pray with my hands held up high.

May the love for my Lord know no boundaries.

May I be the bridge for my Lord's devotees.

May I lay my life over the ocean

As Your devotees cross my Lord.

May I be of help

As You reach Your devotees my Lord.

May my test of faithfulness be nothing

Compared to the love for my Lord.

May I, my Lord's truest devotee, live my life in

DEVOTION OF MY

LORD.

THE OMNIPOTENT AWAITS

My Lord The Omnipotent,

I ask forgiveness for the sinners.

May they be awakened

From their deep sleep my Lord.

May they know of their sins my Lord.

May they ask for forgiveness my Lord.

May they know whom

To ask forgiveness from, my Lord.

May they know

Of their Creator up in Heaven, my Lord.

I pray with my hands held up,

"Oh children of my Lord, ask, seek, and knock,

For my Lord walks the Earth.

With forgiveness,

THE OMNIPOTENT

AWAITS."

YOUR TRUE DEVOTEE MY LORD

My Lord The Omnipotent, The Omnipresence,

As dawn breaks into the night sky,

Let my day

Begin with hope just like

Your morning shining through the vast sky.

Let this day

Bring mercy from my Lord

Unto every household.

Let my mind, body, and soul

Be purified through Your blessings my Lord.

Let my hands

Only be in devotion of You, my Lord.

Let my eyes only see You, my Lord.

Let my ears

Only hear, of Your words my Lord.

Let my lips

Only utter prayers for You, my Lord.

Let my feet

Only be on Your Path my Lord.

As nightfall approaches,

Let my mind, body, and soul

Return Home for I am

YOUR TRUE DEVOTEE

MY LORD.

YOUR PATH MY LORD

My Lord The Omnipotent,

I seek forgiveness in You from all sins.

My Lord, I travel upon a road

Which is made of sins.

My Lord, sins have turned humans into mountains.

My Lord, they stand all around like stones.

My Lord knocks, asks, and seeks on all doors.

My Lord, Your creation have closed

All the doors for blessings.

My Lord, I, Your true devotee, walk on Your Path.

My Lord, I shall knock on every door for You.

My Lord, I shall ask of Your children

To remember their Creator.

My Lord, I shall seek all of Your true devotees.

My Lord, guide me, walk with me,

Stand by me when I walk on Your Path.

My Lord, may Your creation join us on This Path.

Forgive the sins

Of those whom knock, ask, and seek on
YOUR PATH MY LORD.

MY LORD
THE ALMIGHTY,
THE OMNIPOTENT

My Lord The Almighty,

I seek forgiveness in You from all sins.

My Lord The Almighty,

I seek peace in You from all that is unsettled.

My Lord The Almighty,

I seek the truth in You from all that is lost.

My Lord The Almighty,

I seek just in You from all that is unjust.

My Lord The Almighty,

I seek mercy in You from all the punishment.

My Lord The Almighty,

I seek protection in You from all that is evil.

My Lord The Almighty,

I seek The Right Path within You

From all direction.

My Lord The Almighty,

I seek for my Lord The Omnipotent within You

For You are

MY LORD

THE ALMIGHTY,

THE OMNIPOTENT.

CLIMB THE STAIRS OF HEAVEN

My Lord The Merciful,

My Lord The Punisher,

We seek only of You.

My Lord The Most Forgiving,

My Lord The Collector of Sins,

Forgive our manifested sins.

My Lord The Most Loving,

My Lord The Only Teacher,

Teach us from The Book of Life

For we have gone astray.

My Lord The Creator,

My Lord The Sustainer of Life,

Guide us onto Your Blessed Path.

My Lord The Final Judge,

My Lord The Final Destructor,

Allow us to be on Your Boat

For End of Time is but upon us.

My Lord, allow us,

The blessed children of The Omnipotent,

To

CLIMB THE STAIRS OF

HEAVEN.

HOLY CHAPEL OF THE OMNIPOTENT

My Lord The Omnipotent,

Forgive me for my manifested sins.

My Lord The Omnipotent,

The burden of my sins pulls me down.

My Lord The Omnipotent,

The weight of my sins pulls me back.

My Lord The Omnipotent,

The imprint of my footsteps

Have shadows of the Beast.

My Lord The Omnipotent,

With my teardrops

I create a new path toward my Lord.

My Lord The Omnipotent,

My path leads me to the ocean of forgiveness.

My Lord The Omnipotent,

For You, I shall cross the ocean of forgiveness.

My Lord The Omnipotent,

As I cross the ocean of forgiveness,

I arrive at The House of my Lord,

One and only,

HOLY CHAPEL OF

THE OMNIPOTENT.

FASTING FOR MY LORD THE OMNIPOTENT

My Lord The Omnipotent,

With my faith steadfast as ever,

I embark upon Your journey.

With my hands in meditation,

My body in complete devotion,

I walk upon Your journey.

With open eyes and widespread hands,

I look for Your devotees

As my heart guides me to You.

My Lord, pick me up from this road

And make this journey Your Path.

I, the traveler, join all of Your travelers

In devotion.

My mind, body, and soul

Search not for food, money, or housing,

But just for You.

I seek for my Lord,

As my soul is in devotion,

FASTING FOR MY LORD

THE OMNIPOTENT.

EMBRACE OF MY LORD THE OMNIPOTENT

My Lord The Omnipotent,

As dawn breaks on this day,

Protect me from all that is evil.

Protect me my Lord

From the evil around and within myself.

My Lord, keep me safe within Your hands

Away from all the sins

Around, above, and beyond me.

My Lord The Omnipotent,

May Your blessings burn all the temptations

That come my way.

May the day be filled

With peace and serenity my Lord.

May I be celibate from all that is forbidden.

As nightfall approaches, may my love for You

Keep all the forbidden dark sins

Of the unknown forest away.

May I, Your true devotee,

Always embark my life within the

EMBRACE OF MY LORD

THE OMNIPOTENT.

OMNIPOTENT'S TUNNEL OF LIFE

My Lord The Omnipotent,

We, the children of Your world, call upon You.

My Lord, bless Your lost children.

My Lord, guide Your needy children.

My Lord, forgive Your sinful children.

My Lord, help us as our body is sinful,

But our soul is pure and clean.

My Lord, may my teardrops wash away my sins.

My Lord The Omnipotent,

My soul searches only for You.

My Lord The Most Loving,

My heart aches only for You

As my destiny is my Lord's Merciful Path.

My Lord's mercy is our means

And my Lord's Earth is our shelter.

My Lord, bless us so we never falter in our ways.

My Lord, hold us so we never fall off Your Path.

My Lord, watch over us so

We may find our way back Home.

My Lord, may our faith and belief hold us up

As we cross The

OMNIPOTENT'S

TUNNEL OF LIFE.

DEATH KISSES GENTLY FOR DEATH IS KIND

Death kisses gently for death is kind.

Death comes over within our lifetime.

Oh my Lord.

Oh my Lord.

Oh my Lord,

My entire life just passed by within a blink.

Time waits not at my door as death stops by.

My Lord, I smell the wonderful breeze of death

As my windows and doors open welcoming him.

Oh my Lord,

May my soul fly over within the peaceful wind,

When it is my time.

May I be gentle.

May I be kind.

May I be brave when the wind blows the chimes

To announce my time.

My Lord forgive me.

My Lord forgive me.

My Lord forgive me,

For I carry the burden of my sins.

My sinful body is ashamed and heavy

For the flight.

My sinful body is a burden for my soul.

My heart, filled with eternal grief, howls

For my Lord.

My Lord, may my body be sin free.

My Lord, may my soul be free

From all Earthly sins.

My Lord, may I be forgiven before my last breath.

My Lord, may I cross the bridge

Within Your arms, within Your guidance,

Blessed amidst Your love.

May I be amongst Your true devotees my Lord,

For I know as the day ends,

Dark nights will take over.

My Lord, amidst all the darkness,

May Your tunnel of light guide me.

My Lord, I place my hands together

For my last prayer,

Take me Home to The House of my Lord.

My Lord, when The Merciful Angel of Death

Reaches my door for I know then it is my time,

I pray to You, my Lord,

DEATH KISSES GENTLY

FOR DEATH IS KIND.

WORSHIP OF MY LORD

My Lord The Omnipotent,

I only worship You.

My Lord The Omniscience,

May my mind, body, and soul

Always bow down in worship of You.

My Lord The Omnipresence,

May I always be on Your Path.

My Lord, may my path only take me toward You.

My Lord, may the clouds be removed

So my eyes only see You.

My Lord, drown all the sounds around me

So my ears only hear You.

My Lord, even if all the words are lost,

May my lips still utter Your name.

My Lord, when my soul leaves this body,

May my last breath be in the

WORSHIP OF MY LORD.

CHILDREN OF
THE WORLD

My Lord The Omnipotent,

As the nightfall comes and darkness engulfs

All around, above, and beyond,

I, Your devotee, lay my body on this Earthly bed.

My Lord, protect me.

My Lord, protect me.

My Lord, protect me

From the evil all around, above, and beyond.

As the darkness engulfs all around,

I lay my complete faith in You, my Lord

For my faith is believing in

The Oneness of The Omnipotent.

I know my eyes cannot see.

My ears cannot hear the evil forces,

But my Lord's eyes and ears

Protect me from the unknown darkness.

Blind faith I have in my Lord The Omnipotent.

My Lord's shawl covers me

From the cold, winter breeze.

Prayers I recite for my Lord,

Guide me through the dark, freezing nights.

My Lord The Omnipotent watches over me

Throughout the days and nights.

May I, Your devotee, always find my way back

Home through the darkest, starless nights.

May the daylight shine upon me

And guide me through the tunnel of life.

My Lord, may I cross the tunnel of light

In Your protection.

My Lord, guide me, protect me,

And hold me in Your embrace

Throughout my time on this Earth and for eternity.

For I know I shall wake up in Your embrace

As The Door to Heaven opens up

Pouring my Lord's blessings

As daylight breaks through night skies.

It is then protection

Of The Omnipotent shall befall upon all the

CHILDREN OF

THE WORLD.

THE HOLY ARK

My Lord, forgive me for the sins

I carry along with me.

My Lord, save me

From all the natural and unnatural calamities,

And the sins conjoined within them.

My Lord, let there be no sin

Around, above, or beyond me.

My Lord, let the divine halo glow all around me

So I may be in Your divine presence for eternity.

My Lord, may I be amongst the redeemers

Saved by Your divine mercy.

My Lord, let the sinners around me be saved

From their sins by their repentance.

My Lord, may I walk upon The Divine Path

Lighted by Your messengers.

My Lord, accept me upon the abode of

THE HOLY ARK.

MY DEVOTION AND MY MEDITATION

My Lord,

For You, I take this oath.

In complete devotion, I am

For You, my Lord.

My mind, body, and soul are in complete devotion

For You, my Lord.

I solemnly swear I am a devotee

In complete devotion

For You, my Lord.

My mind, body, and soul

Belong only to You, The Creator, The Destructor.

For I am in complete oneness

With my Lord

With whom rest my mind, body, and soul.

Oh The Creator,

Oh The Destructor,

Accept my prayers, my repentance.

Oh my Lord,

Accept

MY DEVOTION AND

MY MEDITATION.

THE MERCIFUL, THE FORGIVER

My Lord, I seek forgiveness in You from all sins.

My Lord, I seek forgiveness for I know

My eyes, my lips, my ears, my hands, my feet,

My mind, body, and soul have sinned.

My Lord, may I be able to restrain from

All known and unknown sins.

My Lord, may my repentance take me to

Your Door of Forgiveness.

May my knock for forgiveness reach

Your Door my Lord.

Oh my Lord, open Your Door of Forgiveness

For I, Your child, want to return

Home with complete faith.

May my sin free mind, body, and soul return

Home to You with complete devotion.

Oh my Lord,

May I be forgiven before my last breath.

My Lord, I know as I knock,

My Lord answers with forgiveness for My Lord is

THE MERCIFUL,

THE FORGIVER.

MY LORD, FORGIVE YOUR CHILDREN

My Lord, forgive me.

My Lord, forgive me

My Lord, forgive me.

My Lord had sent a clean, pure body and I have to

Take this sinful, shameful body back Home.

My Lord, forgive me.

My Lord, forgive me.

My Lord, forgive me.

May I have wisdom my Lord.

May I have energy my Lord.

May I have strength my Lord.

May I find the truth my Lord.

May I see the truth my Lord.

May I be the truth my Lord.

May my nights and days be devoted

In Your worship my Lord.

May my sleep, hunger, and all Earthly needs

Not weaken me.

May I spend my eternity

In Your devotion my Lord.

Forgive me my Lord.

Forgive me my Lord.

Forgive me my Lord.

My Lord, forgive Your children.

My Lord, forgive Your children.

My Lord, forgive Your children.

My Lord, forgive Your children.

My Lord, forgive Your children.

My Lord, forgive Your children.

***MY LORD, FORGIVE
YOUR CHILDREN.***

MY CLEAN AND PURE SOUL

My Lord,

Forgive the sins of this soul.

My Lord The Omnipotent,

Forgive the sins of this soul.

Forgive the sins acquired by this body my Lord.

Frail and tired I walk upon Your Road my Lord.

With sickness and ailing body,

Soring feet, and tired eyes,

I walk upon Your Road my Lord.

For truth, justice, honor, dignity, and courage,

I stand my Lord.

May the words of my Lord

Be my guide and my blessings.

The days may be long my Lord

And the nights longer.

The mornings may seem far away

And the nights never ending,

But I know with my devotion, my belief,

And my faith never failing me,

I shall arrive upon The House of my Lord

As a true devotee.

May The Gates to Heaven open

And welcome me my Lord,

As I bring to The Heavens above

MY CLEAN AND

PURE SOUL.

MAY I BE FREE FROM ALL DEADLY SINS

My Lord, may the sins of the night not touch me.

My Lord, may I find my way in the dark.

My Lord, may the darkness

Not engulf me all around.

My Lord, may the cold night not tempt me

For a warm bed amongst the sinners.

My Lord, may all temptations

Be kept away from my path.

My Lord, darkness engulfs

Even deeper throughout the night.

May I follow Your stars

Through the dark, sinful night.

May Your stars give me hope my Lord.

May the guiding lights keep

All temptations away from me.

Freezing, shivering, wet night it may be,

But my Lord, may this soul

Feel the warmth from The Heavens above.

May the blankets from Heaven cover my body.

May the blankets keep sin away from my body.

May the blankets cover Your creation my Lord.

My Lord throws warm cozy blankets

Through the dark, starless night as sinners walk.

May the blankets cover all,

From the sinners to the pure devotees my Lord.

May I shine The Path with hope

From Your guiding lights.

May I direct Your creation through

The dark, starless, fearful, temptatious night.

My Lord, may I be forgiven and may I find You

Amongst all these sinful, temptatious sins.

My Lord, may I be free from all deadly sins.

My Lord, may I be free from all deadly sins.

My Lord, may I be free from all deadly sins.

My Lord, throughout this dark, temptatious night,

May I be free from all deadly sins.

May I be free from all deadly sins.

May I be free from all deadly sins.

May I be free from all deadly sins.

May I be free from all deadly sins.

May I be free from all deadly sins.

MAY I BE FREE FROM

ALL DEADLY SINS.

TONIGHT

My Lord, protect me from Satan and all evil.

Let no evil enter me or my house at any time.

I rest my faith in You as I rest my soul on this

Earthly bed

TONIGHT.

LIGHTHOUSE OF MY LORD

My Lord The Omnipotent,

Guide me and all of my ways.

May I be protected by Your truth my Lord

For my last breath is but upon me.

Help me my Lord

For I am but lost.

Show me the truth of the unknown

For all is but lost to this world my Lord.

Pull me up my Lord

For the cold, shivering, unknown death

Is but drowning my last lights.

All the lost religions from all around history

Are but claiming Your name my Lord.

May I not be lost amongst them

For I call upon You, my Lord.

May my Lord's Ark pick me up

From the cold dark night's ocean.

May my soul be guided even in this dark ocean

By The

LIGHTHOUSE OF

MY LORD.

DEADLY SINS OF THIS WORLD

My Lord, forgive this sinful soul.

My Lord, forgive the sins of yesteryears.

My Lord, tired and frail,

This soul has been crying for eternity.

May this day bring forth forgiveness

From my Lord to this old soul.

May the repentance of this soul

Be accepted my Lord.

May today bring forth faith, justice, and peace

Upon this sin free soul.

Yesterday, today, and tomorrow,

May I always be Yours my Lord.

May I never go astray from the ways of my Lord.

My Lord, as the Heavenly water of life

Pours all over Your lands,

Washing the deadly sins away,

May we be amongst the ones washed and clean,

Not the ones washed away amongst the

DEADLY SINS OF

THIS WORLD.

ACCEPT MY REPENTANCE

My Lord, it is the burden of sin

That I carry on my shoulders,

For it is why my shoulders crouch in shame.

My Lord, I have wronged.

My Lord, I have wronged.

My Lord, I have wronged.

May I find the right and never wrong again.

Wash away the sins my Lord

So, I may come Home as a redeemer,

Free from all the sins of this soul,

Free from all the sins of this soul,

Free from all the sins of this soul.

My soul repents.

My mind, body, and soul repent.

Accept my repentance my Lord.

Accept my repentance my Lord.

Accept my repentance my Lord.

Accept my Lord

For this tired, old soul repents in Your name.

My Lord, show me The Right Path.

My Lord, be my Guide.

My Lord, be my Guide.

My Lord, be my Guide.

My Lord, accept my repentance.

My Lord, accept my repentance.

My Lord,

ACCEPT MY

REPENTANCE.

PROTECTION OF OUR LORD THE OMNIPOTENT, THE ALPHA AND THE OMEGA

My Lord The Omnipresence,

Protect us from all the evil

Within, around, above, and beyond us.

My Lord The Omnipresence,

Keep us safe from all the deadly diseases

And famine that is destined to come.

My Lord The Omnipresence,

Protect us from

All the natural and unnatural disasters

That are but approaching us.

My Lord The Omnipresence,

Keep us within Your hands

As the foreseen calamities

Are but to come upon us.

My Lord The Omnipresence,

When the world but ends,

May we, Your true believers, be upon

The Merciful Ark of our Creator The Omnipotent.

My Lord The Omnipresence, we know

We are but safe within the

PROTECTION OF

OUR LORD

THE OMNIPOTENT,

THE ALPHA AND

THE OMEGA.

THE GARDEN OF EDEN

Lost, frail, and tired,

I know all but began with You, my Lord

And all shall end but with You.

From the beginning to the end,

I, the lost soul, ask of You, my Lord,

My Lord forgive me.

My Lord forgive me.

My Lord forgive me.

May I but be found within Your mercy.

May I but find You within my search.

May I not be amongst the lost.

As my Lord arrives, I but wait.

Find me my Lord.

Show me my Lord.

Guide me my Lord.

Amongst the lost, I but am.

Amongst the found, I shall be.

For my Lord arrives,

For my Lord arrives,

For my Lord arrives to carry all of the creation.

For You shall take all of

Your creation back Home,

Who but want to be found,

Who but want to be saved,

Who but want to be amongst the pure.

May I, my Lord, the lost soul be found.

My Lord, I ask of You,

Is it time I but come back Home?

Lost I was, but my Lord comes

And I know with my Lord's arrival,

Found I shall be amongst the true devotees.

For my final resting place shall be

THE GARDEN OF EDEN.

I THE SINNER REPENT, REPENT, REPENT

My Lord, we the creation are but lost
In this vast ocean of sins.
We float amongst the sinners.
We dwell amongst the sins.
We hide within the dark, deep ocean
Under the thick blanket of sinners.
My Lord shines the moon upon us
And brings the sun with so much heat.
It but warms our bed of water.
The ocean flows from land to land,
Floods home to home, house after house,
Drowning all of us the sinners.
Within all this, we still hide.
We run from our fate.
We carry our sins along with us.
We drown ourselves in the vast ocean

For all around we see is the ocean of sins.

My Lord comes with The Ark.

My Lord sends life jackets

With various messengers.

My Lord shines the ocean with The Lord's Angels.

My Lord searches for us amongst the sinners.

My Lord cries, "Come to Me."

I hear You, my Lord.

I see You,

But I am so heavy with the burden of sins,

I am drowning.

My Lord, hold me, pick me up.

I give You my hands my Lord.

Take my hands my Lord.

Take me back Home my Lord.

I am but a small fish in this ocean

Drowning in shame,

Repenting, repenting, repenting.

I have lost my ways.

I have lost my path.

I have come far from Home,

Searching for a way out my Lord.

Guide me, show me,

Shine the stars upon my path my Lord.

My Lord, forgive me.

My Lord, forgive me.

My Lord, forgive me.

My Lord's Ark comes and picks up this small fish

Within my Lord's hands gently

And carries me back Home

For I repeat,

I the sinner shall not sin.

I THE SINNER REPENT,

REPENT, REPENT.

THE WINDS OF SIN

My Lord, my Creator,

May I, Your creation, have endurance.

My Lord, my Creator,

May I have patience.

My Lord, my Creator,

May I have courage.

My Lord, my Creator,

As all but get lost,

As all but go astray,

May I then have endurance, patience,

And the courage

To stand against

THE WINDS OF SIN.

THE OMNIPOTENT IN DISGUISE

Oh my Lord, oh The Omnipotent,

Oh my Creator, oh The Omnipotent,

It is but dark, it is but chilly.

As the nightfall begins,

We Your creation, human, animal, and all

Return Home for safety.

My Lord, Your Angels from Heaven but guide us

From dusk to dawn,

Roaming around, keeping all but safe.

Astray we go not, faithful we are always.

Fearful we stay not.

Your Angels protect us from above and beyond.

My Lord, the dark nights also bring to light

The beast, the demon of the dark, dingy night.

My Lord, they are but hunters walking amongst

Your creation, taking but lives for their pleasures.

For their comfort,

They take our sisters and brothers.

For their numbers,

They create their own, using but Your creation.

My Lord, guide us.

Keep us safe in the dark, dingy night.

May we find The Angels of our Lord

Roaming around.

May we embrace Your guiding stars,

Your twinkling lights, Your Angels in disguise.

May we not be fooled and embrace

The demons, the beast, the evil lurking around

To take but another soul and turn them evil

Into the spirits of the dark, dingy nights.

May we be embraced amongst

The Angels of our Lord.

May we be embraced within our Creator

Who walks amongst the humans, the animals,

And all above, on, and beyond,

THE OMNIPOTENT

IN DISGUISE.

THE DEADLY SIN OF TEMPTATION

My Lord The Creator,

My Lord The Sustainer,

My Lord The Destructor,

My Lord The Merciful,

The Merciful, The Merciful.

May I, Your creation, be within Your protection

From all deadly sins.

May I never go astray.

May the sin of wind chimes not reach my ears

For I only hear Your words my Lord.

May my eyelids protect me from the vision

Of temptations as my eyes only see You, my Lord.

May my lips only worship You and Your words

For my lips shall never utter anything

But Your name my Lord.

May my heart never know to punish

Or take revenge, but be filled with love and mercy

For my Lord You are The Merciful.

May my hands never engage in any sins,

For they shall be entwined within prayers for You

And washed by prayers for You, my Lord.

May my feet always follow

Your footprints my Lord.

The Path You have created,

May I walk only on This Path for it is there

And then I shall find You, my Lord.

From my first breath to the last,

May the deadly sins not touch me.

As with each and every breath,

I take only Your name my Lord.

I worship only You, my Lord.

I ask forgiveness only from You, my Lord.

From this Earthly birth to this Earthy death,

If I am to be free from only one sin,

My Lord, may it be from

THE DEADLY SIN OF

TEMPTATION.

THE GATES OF HEAVEN

My Lord, my Creator,

Sin is but in the past.

Repentance is but the present.

Forgiveness is the future.

For this day, this hour, this minute,

What is known as the present,

Today my Lord, I repent, repent, repent.

My Lord, accept my repentance.

My Lord, my soul cries only to You

As I confess my sins and repent, repent, repent.

May my Lord accept the repentance

Of my inner soul

For I walk only for You.

I am but Your creation my Lord

For You are my Creator.

With all my faith, I know my Lord

Awaits my arrival for I am the repenter.

I know my Lord waits with open arms,

For my Lord says, "Knock, seek, and ask."

I knock, seek, and ask,

My Lord, accept my repentance.

With complete faith,

I walk through Your Door of Repentance

To The House of my Lord through

THE GATES OF HEAVEN.

THE GATES OF HELL

My Lord The Merciful,

My Lord The Forgiver,

Oh my Lord, my Lord, my Lord.

Oh The Final Judge of The Judgment Day.

Oh my Lord, my Lord, my Lord.

May I walk out of my grave with hands

In salutation toward only You, my Lord.

May I the redeemer be awakened with redemption

As I cross on to the final stage my Lord.

May I not worry about myself

As I walk through the final field,

But stay in prostration toward You, my Lord.

May my repentance hold me up against all

Temptation, forbidden sin, and the sinners

As they joyfully cross into Hell my Lord.

Oh my Creator,

Oh The Final Judge of The Judgment Day,

With hands in salutation,

Head in prostration,

My mind, body, and soul

I give completely to You, my Lord.

For it is on this day, this time, and this hour

Only known to You,

I watch the sinners one by one fall

Off the bridge into the pits of Hell.

May my feet not fall through

THE GATES OF HELL.

ACCEPT MY SALUTATION MY LORD

My Lord of Heavens and my Lord of Earth,

My Lord of the sinners,

My Lord of the pure,

Accept my salutation my Lord.

I salute only You, my Lord.

I ask of forgiveness only from You, my Lord.

I repent only to You, my Lord.

I ask The Creator's intervention

So, I may not be blinded by the sunlight.

I ask The Creator's help

To keep me safe throughout the darkness.

I ask for The Destructor's blessings

Throughout all the destruction.

I ask of The Destructor to keep me in Your hands

When all is but about to be destructed.

Oh my Lord of all that is and all that is not,

Accept my salutation my Lord,

Accept my salutation my Lord,

ACCEPT MY

SALUTATION MY LORD.

THE ARK OF MY LORD

Let not me be tempted.

Let not I attempt.

Let not there be any sin committed

By me my Lord.

For all around, I see is sin.

All around the air, the sky, the ground, on, above,

And beyond me is smogged up with sin my Lord.

The dark night's sin has polluted the air

Which is but drowning me my Lord.

I feel the waves of sin piercing through my skin,

Through this cold, winter's night my Lord.

The vast ocean of sinful sins all around is

But drowning me my Lord.

I shall fearlessly attempt to find the stream of

Pureness in this dark night's sinful ocean my Lord.

There is but a glass barrier made out of sin

Between You and me my Lord.

May my prayers of repentance pierce through

And break this barrier my Lord.

I see a stream of light piercing

Through the glass my Lord.

I attempt to break the glass of sin

With my redemption my Lord.

I float above the water,

For I am the redeemer floating

Above the ocean of sins my Lord.

I must repent, redeem, and awaken

To break the glass barrier

Between my Lord and myself.

Alone, lost, and drifted I might feel.

Even yet, I know I must awaken first my Lord.

For it is then, I can awaken all the others

From this deep devotional sleep of sin my Lord.

With this newfound awakening and complete faith,

I call upon my Lord.

I feel the glass barrier shatter

And the pure glass of water wash

And bathe me my Lord.

Finally, I see my Lord's Ark of Angels

Bring forth my Lord.

As I reach out, my Lord is there.

As I ask for direction, my Lord is there.

As I seek for attention, my Lord is there.

As I knock, my Lord picks me up

From the dark ocean of sins onto

THE ARK OF MY LORD.

TEST FOR US
THE CREATION

Oh the repented souls,

Come upon The Bridge of Repentance.

The Door of Mercy

But welcomes all of whom

Have but gone through the ocean of sins,

Only to awaken to the blessings of repentance,

The only weapon we have

As we journey through this life

Which is but a

TEST FOR US

THE CREATION.

THE RIVER OF HEAVEN

My Lord, save me.

My Lord, awaken me.

My Lord, guide me

The repenter, the redeemer, the awakened.

My Lord, may we be awakened

From the sinful traits of the human soul.

May my soul know the truth, the complete truth.

May my soul be selfless,

And always be above the sinful traits.

It is but the sinful traits that drown a soul.

As I am drowning, I see not myself

For my mind, body, and soul are but corrupted

By the sins.

My Lord, hold my hands.

Pull me up above the sinful traits

Of the human soul.

I know self-pity, anger, selfishness, hatred,

And resentment drown the soul my Lord.

Hold me, wash me with Your blessings.

Pour Your blessings over me.

Coat me with Your blessings,

So all these sinful traits

Of the sinful soul wash away.

As I float away from the river of sins,

May I always float sin free through

The valleys of the river of Heaven.

May my sins be washed away.

May my sins be washed away.

May my sins be washed away

As I ride the boat and float sin free

Through the valleys of

THE RIVER OF HEAVEN.

FOREVER YOURS
MY LORD

My Lord, forgive the sins.

My Lord, accept the repentance.

My Lord, give us Your protection.

My Lord, give us the direction.

We ask my Lord and we seek and we knock.

My Lord answer.

My Lord answer.

My Lord answer.

Until my last breath,

I shall call upon You, my Lord.

All the strength, all the might,

And all the powers cannot keep me away

From You, my Lord.

The only thing that shall make this body stop

Calling upon You, my Lord, is my last breath

For as I leave this body, I shall still be

Yours my Lord.

For I take the vow,

This mind, body, and soul belong only to You.

My Lord, give me courage.

Give me wisdom.

Show me the path.

Show me the way, so I may be on

Your blessed journey.

For every breath I take is

For You in Your name my Lord.

Every heartbeat that keeps me going is

For You, my Lord.

The day, the time, that but shall arrive

When all of Your creation will be no more,

May this creation be Yours even in death.

A bond between the parents and child

Never breaks even in death.

This creation belongs only to You, my Lord.

I raise my hands in salutation.

I prostrate only to You.

I worship only You

For my mind, body, and soul

Belong only to You, my Lord.

I am Your creation

Who waits upon Your Path,

Hands held up high in salutation,

Mind, body, and soul in prostration,

Counting each day and each night

For I know the time comes upon me.

My Lord, my Lord, my Lord,

As the time ends when all of this shall be no more,

Even then, may this creation always be

Forever Yours my Lord.

May I be Forever Yours my Lord.

FOREVER YOURS

MY LORD.

FORGIVENESS, MERCY, AND BLESSINGS

Oh my Lord,

May there be

Forgiveness, mercy, and blessings

On my plate.

Oh my Lord,

May my repentance be accepted.

Oh my Lord,

May I the redeemer be awakened.

Oh my Lord,

May there be

FORGIVENESS, MERCY,

AND BLESSINGS.

ACCEPT MY PRAYERS

My Lord, lead me away

From nothingness to the pure essence of God.

My Lord, lead me away

From the dark into the light.

My Lord, lead me away

From temptation into The House of Redemption.

My Lord, pull me away

From the wrong and drop me amongst the right.

My Lord, throughout my trials and hardships,

Give me strength and courage.

My Lord, hold my hands throughout eternity.

My Lord, throughout eternity

From dawn to the dark times,

May I not be lost in the ocean of sins.

My Lord, may my drop of sin

Not pollute the ocean.

My Lord, may the polluted ocean not drown me.

My Lord, separate me

From the sinners and place me amongst the pious.

My Lord, may I wash off the sins

Of my mind and body, so my soul

Remains pure and clean.

My Lord, pull me up

From the ocean of sins into the abode of my Lord.

My Lord, may I be the repenter,

The redeemer, the awakened soul.

My Lord, accept my repentance.

My Lord, accept my redemption.

My Lord, accept my awakening.

My Lord,

ACCEPT MY PRAYERS.

THE WORDS OF MY LORD

My Lord, forgive.

My Lord, forgive.

My Lord, forgive.

Let these hands not sin.

Let these eyes not sin.

Let these lips not sin.

Let these ears not sin.

Let this mind, body, and soul not sin.

Let these feet not land upon sin.

My Lord, forgive.

My Lord, forgive.

My Lord, forgive.

When this mind, body, and soul

Reach the land of sins,

My Lord, let me be protected within Your bounds.

Oh my Lord, hear my prayers.

Let this mind, body, and soul be awakened.

Oh my Lord, I live amongst sinners.

I live amongst sin.

I walk amongst sin.

Let me hold on to You

And be Your true, faithful devotee.

Let me be Yours and only Yours.

Let me find my way back to You.

Amongst the sinners I am,

But pure I am.

I stand upon the land of sins,

But I stand sin free.

I stand amongst the ignorant,

But I am the redeemed as

I call upon You.

All around me, sinners walk.

I know of the truth,

But they are flooding me with their lies.

I know the truth,

But they are drowning me amongst their lies.

My heart knows You are there,

But their words are drowning me.

May I be strong.

May I have the courage to announce the truth

Amongst the ignorant.

Alone I walk, frightened I am,

But on this journey, I have my faith

And my love for my Lord and the truth,

The unknown, untold truth,

The veil The Lord has created

To separate Heaven and Earth.

I know I must walk for You, my Lord.

With my faith and love, I shall be strong.

I know my Lord is there when I fall.

I know my Lord is there

When I am but put down by the humans.

Their sharp tongues, their knowledge of nothing,

And their voices of wrong are but loud.

I look at them walking and I know

Their empty vessels make so much noise.

I carry the love of my Lord.

I know this journey is hard,

But at the end, my Lord is there.

Oh my Lord, I ask of You not for anything,

But give me strength, wisdom,

Your love, and courage.

Even alone, may I worship only You

Until my last breath.

When my breath is no more,

May my soul still only worship You,

For the words I leave behind are

But all my love for my Lord.

Mouth to mouth, ears to ears,

My words shall take voice.

My words shall take form of love, multiply,

And shall be

The words of my Lord.

The words of my Lord.

THE WORDS OF

MY LORD.

THE OMNIPOTENT

My Lord, as darkness but approaches,

The night yet is but so long.

Morning star seems but so far away.

My Lord, my Creator, my Protector, my Savior

Forever bless this soul.

Bless this human.

Bless this creation of Yours.

I ask for guidance my Lord.

I knock for answers and I seek only for the truth

For this dark night is so long,

Yet my faith, my belief is so strong.

These human eyes do not see the morning light,

But I know it is there.

These human eyes do not see beyond the darkness,

But I know the twinkling lights but appear.

These human minds do not know beyond,

But I know You are there.

These human ears do not listen to anything,

But our own words,

But I know the words of my Lord but surround us.

I know the words of my Lord but guide us.

I know my Lord's voice but calls on to us.

This human creation sees only

What is in front of us,

But I know my Lord is there.

For it is not what I see,

But what I do not see.

Faith is believing not questioning,

For where there is faith, there is a way.

The Path to my Lord is created upon faith.

Upon embracing faith, my Lord but appears.

The unknown becomes known.

The darkness that evolved all around

But disappears.

Dawn breaks open.

The sun embraces the world.

Your message and messengers,

Your Angels of Heaven,

Your guidelines for us

Are but clear upon the vast sky.

It is then our Lord appears and

Knocks,

Asks,

And seeks

For devotees.

From door to door,

Our Lord knocks, asks, and seeks,

For it is the hour, the time, and day

I await my Lord.

May I, Your devotee, be there

With hands up in salutation,

Mind, body, and soul in devotion.

May I embrace the truth, the whole truth,

And nothing but the truth,

My Lord,

The Omnipotent,

The Omnipotent,

THE OMNIPOTENT.

MY LORD, MY CREATOR

Oh my Lord, my Creator,

This world but fights.

This world but argues.

Oh my Lord, my Creator,

From the beginning to the end, all are but lost.

All find You, yet again, all but lose You.

All see You, yet then become blind.

All hear You, only to be deaf afterwards.

Throughout all of this my Lord, my Creator,

Your name is but lost.

Your Path is but hidden.

I wait within all of this for I know,

Truth leads me to Your Path.

I hear You amongst all that is good.

I see You amongst all that is pure.

For there is only one name,

For I am Your creation, You are

MY LORD, MY CREATOR.

PATH TO HEAVEN

Oh my Lord, my Creator,

May Your protection be upon us the creation.

With mind, body, and soul,

We search for You.

Within the endless skies,

We search for You.

Amongst the vast ocean,

We search for You.

Roaming around the mountain top,

We search for You.

Amongst our kind, warm hearts,

We feel You.

From our soft-spoken words,

We hear You.

Within all race, color, and religion, You appear.

Oh my Lord, for there is but one Creator.

Oh my Lord, for there is but one Judge.

Oh my Lord, may we the creation

Not but divide You The Omnipotent

Into different religions,

For our knowledge is but limited.

May we the creation find and be upon

The Ark of The Omnipotent.

You, my Lord, have but created

The lands, the oceans, the skies,

Of all but whom know Your identity.

As the sun bows down only to You,

The moon but salutes only You.

The stars are there guiding all of Your creation.

Oh my Lord, may we the creation be blessed.

May the blessings of The Merciful be upon us,

For we know our Lord is there.

The Path to our Lord is there.

For with this knowledge,

May we the creation not divide but unite,

And carry all of the creation onto The Path.

May we the creation, in union, be upon This Path,

The

PATH TO HEAVEN.

BY THE CANDLES OF HELL

Oh the children of God,

Oh the lost souls,

Oh the sinners, the tempters,

Spare me from the sins.

Your attractive sins,

Your temptatious path,

Your sweet songs of lust

Pull the sinners one by one.

The children of God jump into the pit.

My Lord, may I, Your child, not be mesmerized

By the mesmerizers of sin.

May I see the difference between

The candles of hope and the candles of sin.

May I not fall prey into this fire pit of the sinners.

May I see through the false hope of the sinners,

As they guide, direct, and lead the children of God

Into the sweet, tempting, dark room

Lighted by sin and sinners

Through the one way passage.

Oh my Lord, may I not fall prey

And follow this path.

My Lord, protect me from this fall.

My Lord, may I not enter this room

Which is lighted,

BY THE CANDLES

OF HELL.

THE DEVOTEE

My Lord, my Creator,

With faith and devotion, I have given

My mind, body, and soul completely to You.

Oh my Lord, my Creator,

Let this faith and devotion not go astray,

And not fall prey to the wrong words

Or the wrong path of human temptation.

Let my words and my path

Always be guided by You.

Let this soul always belong to You.

Let this mind always be of Your will.

Let this body be glorified upon Earth through You.

Oh my Lord, my Creator,

Let my mind, body, and soul belong only to You

For I am Your creation,

Known to this world and beyond as

THE DEVOTEE.

FOR MY CREATOR

My Lord, The Creator,

Bless us the creation.

For You, my Lord, I but love.

For You, my Lord, I but live.

For You, my Lord, I but give.

For You, my Lord, I but exist.

For You, my Lord,

I am but blind for I see no race, color, or religion.

For it is You, my Lord,

Who but created all with love.

My love for my Lord is but blind.

My Lord, these Earthly eyes but place

All of Your creation into this Earthly heart.

My Creator loves all of the creation.

This creation loves all of the creation,

FOR MY CREATOR.

THIS DEVOTEE ONLY WORSHIPPED YOU

My Lord, forgive me.

My Lord, accept me.

My Lord, guide me

As I have washed all my sins.

As days pass and nights go by,

My love for my Lord grows.

As all the sins but burn away like ashes,

I get stronger,

Deep in devotion as I only worship You.

I only call upon You.

My calls of prayer shall be heard from Earth

Up to The Heavens above.

My body cares not for pain I must go through.

My body knows it is just a vehicle

Which only worships You.

From dusk to dusk, I worship only You.

As dusk to dusk is no more, I am no more.

The only proof of my existence will be

THIS DEVOTEE ONLY

WORSHIPPED YOU.

ARK OF FAITH

Oh my Lord,

All around me, darkness but evolves.

The skies are but turning dark.

Thunder roars all around the dark, chilling night.

Humans, animals, all alike

Running from this storm.

All but are trying to hide and find shelters.

I wait in this Ark for You, my Lord,

For Your command.

All scream and shout,

"Come on and hide from this danger."

I face this danger as I know it is then

I shall be victorious.

This storm has been brewing

From beginning of time.

All land, all ocean, all the skies are

But Yours my Lord.

All creation of land, ocean, and the skies

Are but Yours my Lord.

Amongst all these storms,

May I never lose faith.

Amongst all this danger,

May I never fall prey.

Amongst all the lost messages,

May I never get lost.

For You, my Lord, I wait.

For You, my Lord, my eyes but search.

For it is only You, my Lord,

My mind, body, and soul but worship.

For You, my Lord,

I but wait in this vast ocean of sins,

Completely sin free,

Free from all temptation.

Wrapping myself up in the blanket of faith,

I, Your devotee,

With all of my mind, body, and soul,

Wait in The

ARK OF FAITH.

ETERNALLY YOURS MY LORD

My Lord The Omnipotent,

Love is but You and me.

Oh my Lord, The Omnipotent,

It is only You I worship,

You I bow down to.

Oh my Lord, for You I give my life,

For You, I live my life.

My Lord, love is nothing but You.

Eternity is only You.

Life is but Your grace.

Each breath is but Your mercy.

Each day is Your giving.

Each night is Your blessing.

As night dawns upon me,

May the blessings of my Lord be there.

Throughout this night until dawn,

Bestow upon us Your blessings.

Oh my Lord, with dawn I only worship You.

Oh my Lord, throughout this day,

I only worship You.

Oh my Lord, as I wait for the night to come

Upon me, and take me into the darkness,

May I, Your devotee, throughout this dark night

Only worship You.

For the night is dark and the days seem darker,

But Your light glorifies me throughout the days

And the dark nights for I know

This devotee worships You throughout eternity.

My Lord, be mine for I am always Yours,

Forever Yours my Lord.

Oh my Lord eternity be.

Let eternal darkness and eternal light surround me.

Throughout this time,

I shall only worship You, for I am

ETERNALLY YOURS

MY LORD.

REST IN PEACE

My Lord, protect me from all the negativity.

My Lord, protect me

From all the negative adversities of life.

For breath is serenity.

For breath is peace.

With each breath my Lord, protect me

From all the negative adversities of life.

For within each breath, may I find serenity.

For within each breath, may I find peace.

For within each breath, may there be forgiveness.

For within each breath, may there be joy.

For within each breath, may there be calm.

For when this breath gives serenity, peace,

Forgiveness, joy, and calm,

Within that breath, I find You, my Lord.

Within that breath, I find You, my Lord.

Within that breath, I find You, my Lord.

My Lord is serenity.

My Lord is peace.

My Lord is The Forgiver.

My Lord is within the calmness of human joy.

My Lord is within each and every breath.

For You, my Lord,

This mind, body, and soul breathe.

May each breath be for You.

May each heartbeat be for You, my Lord

And when this heart beats no more

And there is no breath left in this mind and body,

May this soul belong only to You.

My Lord, may my last breath be taken for You.

Within Your name,

May I find my last resting place.

Within Your arms, may I find the serenity,

And may my mind, body, and soul

Belong only to You, my Lord.

My Creator, may Heaven be my last Home.

For within Heaven, my last Home,

May my mind, body, and soul lie in peace.

May Heaven be my last resting place.

May I be in my Home, my Home up in Heaven.

May my home up in Heaven

Be my last resting place

For I pray my Lord,

Within my Home up in Heaven,

May I, Your creation,

REST IN PEACE.

REPENTANCE

Sins are committed by human

For You, my Lord, are The Forgiver.

Repentance I know firsthand for I too am a sinner.

Burden of the sins lies in the hands of the sinner.

The soul is but pure and clean.

We, the sinners, are but the carriers of the sin.

This sin, the disease that we have landed upon

Is but given for our own doing.

The Lord has given us one gift, the repentance,

For it is known and it was known to The Lord.

We the humans have but committed

From the first sin to the last.

Yet my Lord, You have given us this deed,

This boon, Your blessings as the

REPENTANCE.

ACCEPT OUR REPENTANCE

May our repentance be accepted.

May we not repeat the sins of yesteryears.

Oh my Lord, accept our repentance.

May we not repeat the sins for we have repented.

Now our deeds take us afar from the sinful lies

And deceit of the dark night.

May the alleys not find us a home.

May the path we travel upon be lighted

By Your rules and governed by Your Angels.

May we walk upon Your Path sin free.

Oh my Lord, accept our repentance.

Save us from our sins.

Oh my Lord, may our sins not find us a home

In the darkness, the dark fearful alleys.

May we not roam around in deceit and lies.

May a pebble stone of lie

Not find a house in our heart.

Oh my Lord, may our mind, body, and soul

Be sin free

For we have repented, redeemed, and awakened.

May we not repeat the sins of yesteryears

For we the sin free souls walk upon

Your Roads, Your Path.

May our repentance be accepted.

May we not repeat the sin after our repentance.

Oh my Lord, may this grave sin

Not find a house within us.

May our repentance glow

And show us the way to our Lord.

My Lord, we pray today

May we not repeat the sins after our repentance.

Accept, forgive, and take us Home.

May my repentance be accepted my Lord

And may my heart not deceive me.

May my mind, body, and soul not deceive me,

And may I not repeat the sin after my repentance

For the grave sin takes over,

Overshadows the human soul.

May I be a candle of hope, a candle of light,

A candle for the passerby

In the dark, starless night.

May I be a candle my Lord.

May I burn myself so I show the light to others.

For this fear, this dreadful fear of repeated sin

Is so fearful my Lord, even death but is nothing.

For this I pray for myself.

Anyone who comes after me and travels The Path,

Come oh the creation of my Lord,

Put up your hands in union and let us pray to

The Omnipotent as we light the candles.

Let us be the guide and not let anyone repeat

The sins after they have repented.

Oh my Lord

ACCEPT OUR

REPENTANCE.

THE ETERNAL TRUTH

My Lord, let the words of this prayer be a shower.

Let my sins be washed away.

With this wash,

I, the pious, ask of my Lord for forgiveness.

Oh my Lord, let this wash take away all the sins

From my mind, body, and soul.

May this creation only worship You.

My Lord, may this worship be eternal.

May nothing, no fog, no glass, nor barriers

Come in between You and me

For my Lord, there is only one door,

That is The Door of Repentance.

There is only one path, the path to The Truth.

There is only one truth,

The Omnipotent, The Alpha and The Omega.

The complete truth, my Lord, the eternal truth,

The Omnipotent is but

THE ETERNAL TRUTH.

THE GLAD TIDINGS OF MY LORD

My Lord,

Forgive for I the redeemer awaken

And travel upon The Road

You have bestowed Your blessings upon.

I need not the help of humans,

For I have the blessings of my Lord.

My Lord, forgive.

My Lord, forgive.

My Lord, forgive.

May I the redeemer be upon Your Blessed Path.

My Lord,

May I never go astray.

May my soul always be pure and clean.

May I the awakened

Always walk upon The Blessed Path,

For all I need is my Lord's Path

For This Path always has the blessings of my Lord.

Today, let us not judge the lost souls

For tomorrow, my Lord but judges all.

Tomorrow at my Lord's Court,

My Lord shall pick me up

And bestow the blessings

For all that is and all that is not

But becomes the final court,

The Court of The Judge

For The Final Judgment Day.

On that day, in that court,

I shall stand up strong

For my mind, body, and soul

Belong only to my Lord.

What you know not, my Lord knows.

What you see not, my Lord sees.

For the complete knowledge lies only

Within the hands of My Lord The Omnipotent.

This old soul, this redeemed soul

Belongs only to my Lord.

This redeemer bows down to only You, My Lord.

This awakened soul worships only You, my Lord.

This devotee salutes, bows, worships

Only You, my Lord.

For this, I have no fear.

For this, I am but strong.

For this, I am but awakened.

For this pours the blessings of my Lord,

As rain drops, as snow falls,

Or as heat but strikes.

I am covered within the blankets of blessings

On this day through The Judgment Day,

Throughout eternity.

For this soul is blessed

For I have

THE GLAD TIDINGS OF

MY LORD.

MAY MY LORD'S WILL ALWAYS PREVAIL

May my Lord be my guide.

May my Lord's blessings be my path.

May my Lord's will always prevail.

May my Lord's will always prevail.

May my Lord's will always prevail.

May I be on my Lord's journey.

May I be blessed.

I walk for You, my Lord.

I live for You, my Lord.

MAY MY LORD'S WILL

ALWAYS PREVAIL.

FOR ETERNITY

Oh my Lord,

Forgive me.

Oh my Lord,

Accept me.

Oh my Lord,

Guide me.

Oh Heavenly skies,

Amongst you are but the secrets of Heaven.

Amongst the Earth,

Are but the secrets of the creation.

As the secrets bury all the sins,

May my sins be washed away

Through my repentance.

Oh Mother Earth,

Accept me as a resident on your chest,

For this devotee lights a candle only for my Lord.

Oh Heavenly skies, within your chest,

Wakes up each morning, the biggest star

Which shines light through to all the creation.

This creation holds a candle for my Lord.

This candle shall burn for eternity

Even when I am no more

For it is in worship of my Lord.

Small, tired, frail I am,

But as long as I have breath,

I shall worship my Lord.

This candle shall burn for eternity for my Lord

For I shall be the lighthouse for my Lord.

Oh my Lord, as darkness but takes over,

All but go astray.

This candle shall burn

And this lighthouse, this vehicle,

My body shall become

Your lighthouse, Your guide.

For You, I shall stand strong

And I shall stand in the deep, dark ocean

With my candle guiding Your creation one by one.

I shall ask all to worship only You.

This devotee shall only worship You.

Even if the waves drown me,

My candle shall burn eternally.

This is the candle of my love.

For You, my Lord, I but am.

For You, my Lord, I but live.

For You, my Lord, I but stand.

I stand strong holding this candle,

Safe within my soul,

For no wind shall come, no rain,

No obstacle shall touch me.

Oh my Lord,

Your words I shall spread in the breeze.

Oh my Lord,

Guide me to You.

Oh my Lord,

It is my love for my Lord that but holds

And protects this devotee.

With this, I shall stand strong for eternity.

My Lord,

Forgive me and accept my devotion.

My Lord,

As time and tide but wash away,

This devotee holds the candle,

As it burns for my Lord,

As I worship only You

FOR ETERNITY.

FOREVER I AM YOURS

Oh my Lord, forgive me, guide me,

Protect me, bless me.

Oh my Lord, all around, I see only You.

All around, I feel is but Your love.

I but feel the immense power of Your guidance.

I ask of Your protection.

I seek for Your blessings.

All around I know my Lord but surrounds me.

Even amongst the ocean of sins,

I find my Lord but guides.

All around the sinful ocean,

I find boats floating with my Lord's love.

Where people find sins but polluting the air,

I find my Lord's love but fills the blue sky.

The clouds pass by blessing me,

Washing my feet, hands, and my hair

From the basin of Heaven.

Blessed be as my Lord's blessings

Pour all over me.

My Lord, I but am in immense love.

I am but in deep meditation.

I am but Your true devotee.

I wish to spread this love and devotion

Amongst the creation.

As I talk with You, they call me crazy.

As I sit and fall to the ground in Your devotion,

They call me a liar.

As I walk miles after miles

Singing songs for You,

They shout, throw their rocks, their words,

Their stones at me, trying to prevent me

From singing my songs for You.

They throw me off the cliffs.

They try to stop me for confused they are

And they try to confuse all.

They follow what is their ritual,

Their understanding given to them

By their forefathers.

Oh my Lord.

Oh my Lord.

Oh my Lord,

They divide through different religions,

Yet they do not sing the songs

For my Lord in union.

Oh my Lord, what am I to do.

I see the path and the way for the immense love

You have spread from Heavens above to the Earth.

I shall love them even when they hate me.

I shall guide them even when they want to be lost.

I shall sing for all.

Even when they divide, I shall unite.

I shall walk with my head held up high,

Singing my songs amongst all the creation,

For I know it is they who are but lost,

For I have found You.

I have found Your Path.

I have been guided by You, my Lord.

I shall not fall prey amongst the sinners.

With their stones,

They shall try to change my words,

But death be calm, death be gentle

For even with death, I shall sing my songs for You,

For I know my Lord is there.

I know my Lord stands above the hill,

Hands held up for all of creation to return Home.

I, Your devotee, shall sing for all

As I have found You.

This love I have found is my protection.

This love I have found is my guide.

This love I have found is my way,

And this love I have found is the music

From the flute of my heart.

As I shall play the tunes on the flute,

I shall sing the songs of my love,

For I know Your devotees,

Your creation shall sing.

They may not take my word,

Follow my path, or listen to this devotee,

but my songs written for all of Your devotees,

With love played on my flute are

For Your Creation for You are The One Creator.

As all the children of this world unite,

They shall sing these songs I leave behind

For them to recite.

Through these songs,

Each creation shall but sing,

FOREVER I AM YOURS.

ANGELS IN DISGUISE

From Heavens above, Earth beneath,

Angels walk amongst us invisibly.

Around the darkness, around the pain,

Around all misery and anguish,

Angels appear in disguise.

From Heavens above, Earth beneath,

Angels walk within us.

They appear within us,

And share our struggles, our stories of life.

All of whom see them,

Walk away refusing to take or give a lending hand

As they are known as the strangers.

I see them as they see me.

With a smile, I give them my hands

As these strangers, oh my Lord, are but The

ANGELS IN DISGUISE.

DOVES OF HEAVEN

Oh my Lord, accept my salutation,

Accept my prostration,

For I prostrate only to You.

A sinner I was, but for You, pious I am.

This human has sinned my Lord,

But You are my Lord, my Creator.

Forgive this human soul,

And accept me as Your true devotee.

For You, my Lord,

I have repented.

For You, my Lord,

I have washed all my sins and redeemed.

For You, my Lord,

I go into prostration.

For You, my Lord,

In devotion, I but am.

With my head down in prostration,

Hands in salutation, I am only for You, my Lord.

For this human knows only You, sees only You.

My love is but eternal for You, my Lord.

With this love and this freedom my soul has found,

I know I have but found my Lord.

With this acquired freedom, I feel free.

This soul is free from all the Earthly sins,

For as I prostrate to You, my Lord,

I have given up all worldly desires.

My mind, body, and soul

Belong only to You, my Lord.

Accept me for I am Your true devotee.

Oh my Lord, as I raise my hands in salutation,

As my lips utter this prayer,

May this prayer be my freedom

From all known and unknown sins

This Earthly body but has acquired.

For as I prostrate to You, I feel as if

I have taken rebirth all over again.

Like a newborn child,

I am free of all Earthly sins and bondages.

For my only bond is with You,

My Lord, my Creator.

May this human only worship You.

May my mind, body, and soul,

Every part of my being,

Only worship You.

Even when this Earthly body is no more,

May my mind, body, and soul worship only You.

Oh my Lord, my Creator,

May I be free from all Earthly sins

For it is then this Earthly bondage

Shall be no more.

I have only one bondage

For You are my Creator,

I am but Your creation.

Oh my Lord,

May this prayer be like the white doves of Heaven,

Who are but sin free,

And fly to rescue pure souls from all Earthly sins.

Oh my Lord,

May the remainder of my life be

Guiding Your creation back to You.

Accept this prayer my Lord,

Accept my repentance my Lord.

Accept me my Lord.

For with this prayer, may I be

Like the white

DOVES OF HEAVEN.

LIGHT FOR ETERNITY

My Lord, heal us from all worldly ailments.

My Lord, heal us from worldly blindness.

My Lord, heal us from worldly arrogance.

Heal us from our inner selfishness.

Heal us from all the Earthly, Heavenly sins

That but burn our inner soul.

My Lord, it is then, we shall be able to see.

It is then, we shall heal.

It is then, we shall praise The Lord.

It is then, we shall know our true inner soul.

Oh my Lord, relieve this ailment

From my mind, body, and soul.

Let my soul be pure and clean.

Let my soul be free from all worldly obstacles.

Let my soul be complete.

My Lord, I, Your devotee, call upon You.

May the healing powers of my Lord

Heal me completely.

May I know this soul is but clean and healed.

Oh my Lord, this world is but filled with darkness.

May the light of The Omnipotent shine upon us

And may we never go astray.

Hold these hands my Lord,

For then I shall never fall.

Show my eyes The Path my Lord,

For then I shall never be lost.

Let my ears only hear You, my Lord,

For then no sound shall drown me.

Let my lips utter only Your praise my Lord,

For then I shall know the eternal truth.

May I be the candle that but glows

For Your creation throughout eternity.

May this candle not burn out

For may my Lord's blessings

Keep this candle going for eternity.

Oh my Lord, I am a candle glowing in the dark

For You, for Your creation.

May they see this candle and follow me

For I shall glow for eternity.

For You, my Lord,

I shall burn this candle for eternity.

Let the oil in this candle

LIGHT FOR ETERNITY.

FOUND MY HEAVEN

Oh my Lord, my Creator,

All but say it is Your eternal blessings,

Your eternal peace,

Your eternal love

Where eternity but is found

For within all of this is Heaven.

For me my Lord,

My eternal blessings,

My eternal peace,

My eternal love,

Eternity I have but found

When I but find You.

I search not for Heaven my Lord,

But these eyes only search

For my Lord, my Creator,

For it is then I have but

FOUND MY HEAVEN.

AWAKENED BEFORE ALL BUT ENDS

Oh my Lord, how big the sin is.

How big of a sinner I have become.

The love for my Lord is so weak,

My body but falls asleep.

Oh my Lord, how big the sin is.

How big of a sinner I have become.

The sins of my body burden me

And my body but drowns in my selfish needs.

Where can I find myself, oh my Lord?

How do I find myself?

I wait every day and every night

Upon Your Doorsteps to wake up, to find myself.

All around, all but ask to call upon The Lord,

Ask The Lord for guidance,

Go to The Lord.

I know I must wake up first for it is then

I can find You for this shameful body is sinful.

The sins burden me.

How my Lord, how my Lord shall I face You,

Show You my sins, show You my burden of sins?

My sinful body drowns me in my selfish needs.

I wait upon my Lord's Door.

In fear, I knock not, I seek not,

And I ask not for what is it I say

When my Lord appears?

What is it I show when my Lord is in front of me?

What is it my Lord sees when we finally meet

For I hide all my sins, all my burden

From all so quietly, shamefully.

But my Lord, how do I hide it from You

For You see all, You hear all,

And You shall talk of it when we but meet.

My Lord, I have one prayer,

May I with my sinful soul, shameful body,

And this burdened mind wake up.

May I wake up and may I find myself

Amongst the blessed souls, the blessed minds,

And the blessed bodies,

The selfless humans and Angels,

All of Your creation, human, animal, Earthly,

Heavenly, brothers, and sisters.

May I find myself amongst them,

Your chosen ones

For I know You choose

All of Your creation equally.

All but say Lord's chosen ones,

But You never say anything

For we are all Your chosen ones.

But I choose You, my Lord,

As my complete Savior

For I know there is no one but You.

With You, everything but began.

Within Your commands,

May this sinful body awaken

Before everything but ends.

My Lord, my Creator, my Savior,

With hands held up high,

Head bowed down in prostration,

May this mind, body, and soul

Be awakened before all but ends.

May this mind, body, and soul

Be awakened before all but ends.

May this mind, body, and soul

Be

AWAKENED BEFORE

ALL BUT ENDS.

PROTECT US FOR ETERNITY

Oh my Lord, oh my Creator,

As the day but goes and night but approaches,

We the devotees end up in the darkness.

With hands held up in prayers,

Heads bowed down in prostration,

We the devotees cry only to You

For we know the hardship but lays ahead of us.

The roads are dangerous.

The time is dark for it is called End of Time.

In this hour, on this day,

May we, Your devotees, be guided by You.

But at all times,

We have our heads bowed down in prostration,

Hands held up in salutation.

We cry to You.

May the roads be lighted up with Your messages.

May we see the light of our Lord.

Immersed in devotion,

Heads bowed down in prostration,

Hands held up in prayer,

May we know the truth from the false.

Oh my Lord, oh my Creator,

Oh The Most Merciful, oh The Final Judge,

Pick up Your devotees

As we are stranded in this lost ocean.

May the darkness not evolve all around us

And may we not be lost.

May we find the light that glorifies the dark nights

And twinkles in Your night sky.

May we follow Your twinkles

And end up in Your House,

The House of The Mercy,

The House of The Merciful,

The House of The Forgiver,

The House of The Judge of The Judgment Day.

May we arrive within Your embrace.

May we find ourselves in the embrace

Of our Creator, The Omnipotent.

Oh my Lord, forgive.

Oh my Lord, show us the true path.

Oh my Lord, hold us up within Your hands.

Oh my Lord,

May this darkness not be bestowed upon us,

The sins of the ocean,

For the droplets fall like rain

All around us, on us, above us, and below us.

The droplets of water they are not,

But they are the droplets of sins.

Even they may be washed away by our devotion,

By our prayers of repentance.

For all throughout the dark night,

We pray glory be to my Lord,

For I have the glad tidings of my Lord,

For Your love for us and our love for You shall

PROTECT US FOR

ETERNITY.

I AM BUT YOUR CREATION

Oh my Lord, oh my Creator,

I pray for guidance.

What is a religion?

Is it not You and us the creation?

Is it not the complete union

Between a creation and The Creator?

Oh my Creator,

May I have a direct connection.

Oh my Lord,

May there be no separation between You and me.

For You are my Creator.

I AM BUT YOUR

CREATION.

FOR YOU, MY LORD, I BUT AM

Oh my Lord,

As darkness but evolves all around me,

I search for You within The Heavens.

Oh my Lord,

As darkness but blinds me,

I search for You within the oceans.

Oh my Lord,

As darkness but imprisons me,

I search for You on the Earth.

Above, on, beyond, I search only for You.

My Lord, invisible You have become,

But visible I am to You.

My Lord up in Heaven, my Lord on Earth,

My Lord in between land, ocean, and nothingness,

You are everywhere.

I am visible to You.

It is within Your knowledge where I but am,

But my knowledge lets me worship You

Even though I know not of

Your identity,

Your whereabouts,

Where You are from,

To where You but go.

But my Lord, my path is known to You,

For it is Your Path,

Your footsteps,

Invisible they may be, but I follow.

For Your mountains,

Your skies,

Your oceans,

And Your Earth but guide me.

The whispers of the night sky guide me.

The twinkling stars above in Heaven guide me.

Messengers You have brought upon this Earth

Have built a staircase from Earth to Heaven.

The steps I take one by one

As I step onto this whirlwind that dazzles me.

But with faith, I know I can cross this ocean,

The skies, the Earth, and what is known

And unknown to all that I know,

All is but known to You.

Oh my Lord, invisible You are, visible I am.

This creation calls You day, night,

And throughout the life.

Darkness evolves around me,

But I am not afraid

For I know my Lord is but watching.

For all is known to You

For I have the faith with me on This Path.

My faith blinds me my Lord

And this blind faith that I have

Carries me toward You.

Oh the dark nights,

Dark you may be,

But I have the glory of my Lord's light.

Blessed be.

Blessed be.

Blessed be,

For I know my Lord's glory.

My Lord watches over me throughout the night,

Throughout the day, throughout eternity.

For You, my Lord, I but am.

For You, my Lord, I but am.

FOR YOU, MY LORD,

I BUT AM.

AWAKENED

My Lord, I am the sinner,

But You are The Forgiver.

My Lord, I am naked in front of You

For all is but known to You.

The doors have closed all around me,

But I know The Door of Repentance

Is always open

For I am the sinner

But You are The Forgiver.

I have deceived,

But I have no where else to go my Lord

For I know You are The Forgiver.

As I stand in the shower,

The water washes away the dirt from my body,

But my sins stay in my soul.

My soul cries in pain.

Oh my Lord, I know my sins.

Forgive me my Lord,

For I know my Lord is The Forgiver.

The pain in this body is only physical,

But the pain my soul takes upon is eternal

For the world sees me in clothing,

In attire I can afford to cover my shame,

But my Lord sees the truth beneath this veil

For all is known to You, my Lord.

Oh my Lord,

This day, I open up my wounds

For I know I have but sinned.

Oh my Lord,

Accept my repentance

For I know I have but

AWAKENED.

THE REPENTER

Oh my Lord, this sinner stands in front of You.

Oh my Lord, this sinner stands in front of You

With shame and embarrassment

Above all the pain for I have let down my Lord.

If time finds no space for me,

If my days are but the last days on Earth

As the time is only known to You,

May this repentance be accepted as my last prayer.

I accept the death my Lord, as I accepted the life.

I promised I would never forget The Omnipotent,

But as life came, I forgot all.

But my Lord, let this truth be known.

On this day, I repent as if this is my last day.

I accept all of my punishment

As The Lord has forewarned us.

But my Lord, I ask one thing.

May You be mine for I am only Yours.

This day, I repent.

This day, I redeem

And on this day for You, my Lord,

I have awakened.

For this, repentance be mine

For the sins are but mine.

But my Lord, You are mine

For I am but Your creation.

My Lord, forgive.

My Lord, forgive.

My Lord, forgive,

For I know the difference between

The sinner and pious is The Door of Repentance.

For I know where there is no hope,

There is but one.

For I know my Lord is there.

For I know my Lord is there.

For I know my Lord is there.

For I know I am but this,

THE REPENTER.

DOOR TO MY LORD

I look for You throughout the days.

I look for You throughout the nights.

I look for You at the crossroads.

I look for You at the corners.

I find You throughout the time.

I find You throughout eternity.

My eyes search for You.

My mind drifts all around trying to find the clues.

My Lord, my Creator, oh The Omnipotent

But where do I find You?

My Lord, You have arrived at every corner

When I but fell.

My Lord, You blessed at every crossroad

When I was but lost.

My Lord, You taught me how to walk

When I but lost control.

My Lord, You taught me where to go

When all but became dark

From the skies to beneath the Earth.

My Lord, at this stage, I wait for You

For I know You were always there.

I know You always reached out.

But my Lord, how do I reach out to You?

How do I be there for You?

My Lord, this devotee wants to be there for You,

For my love is You, my Lord.

My life is but Your blessings my Lord.

Each breath I take is but Your gift my Lord.

My Lord, where do I find You?

For my mind, body, and soul, I ask my Lord

How, where, and when shall my eyes see You?

As I touch my heart,

My mind, my body, and my soul know

You have always been here with me.

When I find myself, I know I have found You,

For through my mind, body, and soul, I reach

The

DOOR TO MY LORD.

MY LORD
THE OMNIPOTENT

Oh my Lord, protect us from all evil.

Oh my Lord, protect us from the dark forces

Arriving from the unknown or known.

My Lord, may the darkness not overtake the dawn

For the nights are turning darker

And dawn seems so far away.

The dark creepers are but crawling out

From beneath the graves.

My Lord, the fear of this darkness engulfs all

As it is a smog that grows in the dark.

This smog is becoming a shadow

And is traveling throughout the Earth.

My Lord, the shadows of sins

From beneath the Earth are awakened

And stand upon the lands.

My Lord, give us protection.

My Lord, immerse us within Your embrace.

My Lord, hold us so we the devoted

Do not go astray.

My Lord, may we not be fearful, but brave.

My Lord, may our mouth not clatter out of fear,

But only have Your name on our clattering lips.

My Lord, may I be Your warrior

Who but fights the sins and the sinners.

May the sins and sinners

Not be my friend on this journey of life.

May my life only be for You, my Lord.

For in life or in death,

I am but Yours my Lord.

For this, I am the brave,

The warrior who but shall defeat all evil.

I shall be victorious for You, my Lord.

This life on Earth or beneath

Or above belongs only to You.

On this day, this time, and this hour,

I, Your devotee, give all that I am,

And I was, or shall ever be completely to You.

I surrender all of that I am to You, my Lord,

For I belong only to

MY LORD

THE OMNIPOTENT.

JOURNEY OF MY LIFE

My Lord,

My Creator,

You have but placed us, the travelers,

Upon this journey,

With struggles, agony, pain, health, wealth,

Wisdom, love, and victory

As our companions of life.

May I, Your devotee, the traveler,

Have as my companion only Your blessings

As I embark upon this blessed

JOURNEY OF MY LIFE.

MY LORD, MY CREATOR BUT FINDS ME

Blessed be the name of my Lord.

Blessed be the words of my Lord.

Blessed be the sight of my Lord

For I see You,

Amongst Your creation.

For I feel You,

Within the days

And throughout the nights.

Your footsteps,

Are all over the Earth.

Your blessings,

Flow throughout the oceans.

Your light

Twinkles all throughout the skies.

Your love,

Surrounds me when I am lonely.

Your sunshine,

Hugs me as I shiver with fear.

Your rain,

Showers all over me,

As I have repented, redeemed, and awakened.

I find You all over and know when it is but time,

It is but then,

MY LORD, MY CREATOR

BUT FINDS ME.

BLESSINGS OF THE MERCY

Oh my Lord,

Today give us but the gift of mercy.

For on this day,

I ask of You for mercy.

Where all but is lost,

Where nothing is but found,

Where hearts are but broken

Where nothing but sorrow engulfs,

I ask You, my Lord, for mercy.

My Lord, my Creator,

Let The Bridge of Mercy but appear.

My Lord, let The Bridge of Hope

But shine upon the dark, lost ocean.

My Lord, let this sinner be not lost.

My Lord, may my heart find You

And may this be my awakening.

My Lord, my Creator,

May my heart beat only for You

As I walk upon this bridge.

I know even when all is but lost,

All is but dark,

And all but is fading away,

It is then I find the mercy of my Lord,

In the dark, in the light, always waiting for me.

It was I who but did not see You, my Lord.

It was I who but was lost my Lord.

It was I who but got onto

The wrong boats my Lord.

My Lord, my Creator,

Without a word, a sound, or giving us a glimpse,

Walks silently, gracefully,

With hands shining like the stars,

Feet glowing like the moon,

My Lord walks and leaves upon us,

The

BLESSINGS OF THE

MERCY

BLESSED BE I HAVE THIS DAY, THIS NIGHT, THIS HOUR

Blessed be the day.

Blessed be the night.

Blessed be this life,

For I am still alive.

This time I have, I but repent.

This day I have, I but repent

Blessed be this life.

For all my sins, I but repent.

My Lord, let me not waste a day,

An hour, or a minute,

For the time left for me,

I know of not.

I know my Lord,

The days shall end.

The nights shall pass.

For tomorrow comes for me or not,

All of this is but unknown.

All but is known is the present.

For this time is but a gift to all creation

From the above.

For this my Lord, I take upon my lips a prayer.

I repent, redeem, and awaken.

I repeat all throughout my time,

Blessed be the day, blessed be the night.

Blessed be, blessed be.

BLESSED BE I HAVE

THIS DAY, THIS NIGHT,

THIS HOUR.

THE CANDLES OF MY LORD

Blessed be the hands of the devotees

For we, the devotees,

Carry the candles in our hands.

For the stars may not blink,

And the moon may not shine,

And the sun may not warm us up,

But we, the devotees,

Carry the candles in our hands.

Oh the creation of my Lord,

Wake up, stand straight, and glow

For in your hands, the candles shall blink,

For they shall take you to The Door of The Lord.

For then, you shall become the light,

The star that lights up the sky of my Lord

For where there is a devotee, there is my Lord.

Where the devotee stands, The Lord is but found.

Oh the devotees of my Lord,

Know it whether in the dark

Or within the bright days,

Or when the days are dark and nights are darker,

Or even when the days are bright

And nights are brighter,

Within the dark or the bright,

If there is a devotee, The Lord is but found.

Oh the true devotee,

Know this truth,

This complete truth.

It is within each and every devotee.

It is within your hands.

You carry the candles of my Lord.

Blessed be, blessed be, blessed be,

Blessed be the devotees who but carry

THE CANDLES OF

MY LORD.

MY LORD, PROTECT

My Lord, protect me

From the unknown to the known.

Protect me from the unseen to the seen.

Protect me from the beast,

From the evil,

From the deceivers,

From the humans, animals,

And all that is known, unknown

To the eyes of this human.

For the soul remains protected

For it is in Your hands my Lord.

But my mind and body on this Earth

Need protection my Lord

For I am the biggest deceiver of my own self

For I see not the sinners.

I hear not the sinners.

I feel not the sinners.

But I trust the sinners, the sins,

And the commitments made by the sinners.

Oh my Lord, free me.

Oh my Lord, help me.

Oh my Lord, guide me

For the nights feel dark.

The days feel darker.

My Lord, I am but lost

For this Earth has become an ocean of sins.

The sinners are floating on, above, and beyond.

I walk upon Your Path.

I walk with Your name on my lips.

May I be protected

From the men, from the women,

From the deceivers, from the darkness,

From the evil that roams around

And I see them not.

I feel them not.

But I am lost.

My Lord, protect me.

My Lord, hold me.

My Lord, pick me up

And place me into the hands of The Omnipotent

For I am Yours,

I was Yours,

And I shall always be Yours.

Oh my Lord, protect me

For the days have come to an end.

End of Time but approaches us

And the darkness is coming to erupt all of eternity.

There is only one light

That pours through this darkness,

That guides us like a candle of hope.

I carry a candle of hope in my hands.

Protect me, hold me, guide me my Lord

For this devotee is in danger.

Through this time, through the days,

Through the nights, may I be protected.

My Lord, protect me.

My Lord, hold me.

My Lord, guide me.

For I came upon this world

Through the tunnel of my Lord.

May I go through the tunnel to my Lord.

Only in Your hands,

May my mind, body, and soul rest.

My Lord, protect.

My Lord, protect.

MY LORD, PROTECT.

WE THE CREATION GIVE GRACE

My Lord, protect, preserve, and bless us

Throughout the days and throughout the nights.

May we never go astray.

May the blessings of The Lord befall on us

Throughout the days and throughout the nights.

Blessed be, blessed be, blessed be.

My Lord, may there always be food

Throughout the days and throughout the nights.

My Lord, may we always have a shelter,

A bed, and a blanket to stay warm and dry

Throughout the days

And throughout the cold, freezing nights.

My Lord, bless us for You are The Protector,

The Preserver, The Giver, The Sustainer.

We only worship You.

We only follow Your Path.

May This Path be blessed.

May This Path be blessed.

May This Path be blessed.

Blessed be The Path.

Blessed be The Path.

Blessed be The Path.

My Lord, my Creator,

My Lord The Giver, The Taker,

My Lord The Omnipotent,

Blessed be the days.

Blessed be the nights.

May the grace of The Omnipotent be upon us

Throughout the days and throughout the nights.

Blessed be the grace of my Lord,

May it be upon us,

Throughout the days and throughout the nights.

Blessed be throughout the days

And throughout the nights for You, my Lord,

WE THE CREATION

GIVE GRACE.

LORD FINDS US

My Lord, my Creator,

All around me is anger,

Fury, mistrust, and resentment.

Even the skies roar in anger.

Earth cries out as she splits up the lands.

May there be peace.

May there be serenity.

May there be love.

May we, the humans, look into our own souls

For it is where we shall find peace.

Oh my Lord, oh my Creator,

May my prayer for all humankind be answered.

May we know the complete truth.

May the knowledge be given to us.

May we, the creation, find ourselves first

For then, we shall land upon The Doors of Peace,

The Doors of Serenity,

The Doors of Forgiveness.

For then, may our soul guide us

To the complete inner peace.

Accept our prayers my Lord,

For as we find ourselves first,

It is then our

LORD FINDS US.

BLESSED BE HEAVEN

My Lord, my Creator,

I search for You within the skies.

I see Your eyes watching over,

Keeping me safe from all evil eyes.

I search for You on Earth beneath.

I see my Lord holding on to me,

For it is then, I am but able to walk.

I search for You throughout the blazing desert sun,

Not fearing the burning heat.

I know the winds of my Lord cool my soul,

As the winds blow through the air,

Whispering prayers to keep me going.

I search for You in the deep blue ocean,

As I fear not the waves.

I find my Lord washing my sins away,

As I repent, repent, repent.

At the end of my day, waiting to return Home,

I realize above, around, and beyond me,

All that I see, hear, and feel,

Standing always around me is

My Lord, my Creator.

For I know I have never left Home,

For all of this is,

BLESSED BE HEAVEN.

SIN FREE

My Lord, may I, Your devotee, not sin.

Oh my Lord, even this world is but emerged

Into the ocean of sins and sinners.

Oh my Lord, may I, Your devotee,

Rise above the sins and sinners, pure and clean.

Oh my Lord, even when this mind and body

Are no more, may my soul be sin free.

Oh my Lord, for You in devotion, I but am.

For You my Lord,

I immerse my mind, body, and soul.

For You, I swim in this ocean of sins

And even then, be pure and clean.

Oh my Lord, my Creator,

Hold me within Your embrace,

Away from all Earthly sins and sinners.

May my prayers be accepted my Lord

And up to my last breath, may I, Your devotee, be

SIN FREE.

INVISIBLE HOLY ARK

My Lord, my Creator,

Within Your world, Your oceans, The Ark but is.

The Ark for the devotees

Invisibly swims the oceans all around the world.

She searches with her light and sound,

Searching for devotees.

She carries all the devotees one by one.

My Lord, my Creator,

May I, Your true devotee,

Be amongst one of the blessed to board upon this

INVISIBLE HOLY ARK.

CANDLES OF HOPE

My Lord,

With the sun setting in Your vast sky,

The Earth but is in the dark.

May I, Your devotee,

Be there with a candle in my hand.

My Lord,

As the night sky but turns dark with

Your moon trying to peek through to give us hope,

May I, Your devotee,

Be there with a candle in my hand.

My Lord,

As house after house

But turns dark, searching for light,

May I, Your devotee, be the light bearer

With a candle in my hand.

My Lord,

As Your moon and twinkling stars

Try to send the message of Your sun's birth,

As all but watch out for the birth of Your sun,

May we, the creation,

Await and light up each house one by one

As we carry

The

CANDLES OF HOPE.

ABOUT THE AUTHOR

I am an unknown person who lived the struggles, overcame the obstacles, as I have endured the pain and joy of life as they landed upon my door.

I like to be the unknown face to whom all can relate. I want you to see your face in the mirror when you search for me, not mine. For if it is my face in the mirror, then my friend you see a stranger. The unknown face is there so you see only yourself, your struggles, your achievements as you cross the journey of life. I want to be the face of a white, black, and brown, as well as the love we are always searching eternally for. If this world would have allowed, I would have distributed this prayer book to you with my own hands as a gift from a friend. Please take this book as a message from a friend.

You have my name and know I will always be there for anyone who seeks me. My home is Washington State, USA, yet I travel all around the world to find you, the human with humanity. Aside from my books, I love writing openly on my blog. Through this blog journey, I am available to all throughout this world. Come, let us journey together and spread positivity, as I take you on a positive journey through my blog.

For more information about any one of my books, or to read my blog posts, subscribe to my blog on my website, www.annmarieruby.com. Follow me on social media, @AnnahMariahRuby on Twitter, @TheAnnMarieRuby on Facebook, @ann_marie_ruby on Instagram, and @TheAnnMarieRuby on Pinterest.

I have published four books of original inspirational quotations:

Spiritual Travelers: Life's Journey From The Past To The Present For The Future

Spiritual Messages: From A Bottle

Spiritual Journey: Life's Eternal Blessings

Spiritual Inspirations: Sacred Words Of Wisdom

I have also published a book of original prayers:

Spiritual Songs: Letters From My Chest

I am blessed to also share with you information about my upcoming books:

Spiritual Lighthouse: The Dream Diaries Of Ann Marie Ruby

Spiritual Ark: The Enchanted Journey Of Timeless Quotations

I give you samples from each of my previously published books as I have written these from my heart for all of whom seek the spiritual journey.

My Spiritual Collection

"*Close* your eyes and see the *love* spread throughout this *globe* and as it *lights* up each and all houses, may we open our *eyes* and realize this was a *dream*, but now it is a *reality*."

*Spiritual Travelers: Life's Journey From The Past To The Present For The Future

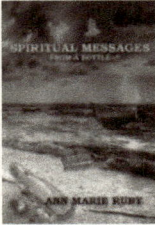

"*The* wind and the windchimes, *singing* the songs of *love*, trying to *unite* the world, they send this *music* through all the open *windows*."

*Spiritual Messages: From A Bottle

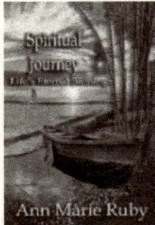

"*Heal* all through the *sweet* songs of *life*, for the *songs* are but *heard* as the *stories* are but *written*."

*Spiritual Journey: Life's Eternal Blessings

"*Songs* are the *sweetest energy* of *life*. They bring to *union* all race, color, and *religion*."

*Spiritual Inspirations: Sacred Words Of Wisdom

My Upcoming Books

Spiritual Lighthouse:
The Dream Diaries Of Ann Marie Ruby

Within the dark, starless, foggy nights, my dreams appeared like the lighthouse always guiding me throughout my life. Dreams are spiritual guidance from the unknown. When the human body but falls asleep, it is then that our spiritual soul guides us throughout eternity. The soul walks into a parallel world where the past and the future exist in the same universe. Walk with me, as my soul but has walked the past and the future all throughout my life. Warnings, dangers, and surprises came upon my door, always guiding me like a lighthouse blinking in the dark night's sky. Alone, lost, and stranded I was until a lighthouse appeared within the ocean of the lost, my blessed dreams.

Take my hands and walk with me along this very personal path, as we journey together through my dream diaries, I call her, *Spiritual Lighthouse: The Dream Diaries Of Ann Marie Ruby*.

"Dreams are given from the Heavens above onto all within the Earth beneath for within them lie the miracles of eternity."

Spiritual Ark: The Enchanted Journey Of Timeless Quotations

Be enchanted throughout this book as you travel through the mystical world of quotations, where my four books of original quotations have now been combined into one complete journey.

In this book, you will travel through time as this spiritual journey of quotations lands upon all souls seeking spiritual guidance and solace through words. Throughout history, words have guided all as she is immortal and lives on beyond time and tide. These original quotations have come from love and peace as they have been written with ink and have taken life from within these pages of history.

May these blessed quotations travel time with you as you take them upon your blessed journey of life. Keep them within your soul as you embark upon this, *Spiritual Ark: The Enchanted Journey Of Timeless Quotations*.

"The enchanted journey through words of wisdom keeps the soul in harmony throughout eternity."

www.ingramcontent.com/pod-product-compliance
Lightning Source LLC
LaVergne TN
LVHW011347080426
835511LV00005B/165